Praise for *Relations*

"*Relationship Essentials* is the essen[...] ship skills that are needed in every important [...] will apply what you learn here to your relationships with fam[...], friends, and coworkers. Practical and user-friendly, this book will significantly raise your relationship IQ."

— **Ron L. Deal**, therapist, speaker, and bestselling coauthor of *Building Love Together in Blended Families* (with Dr. Gary Chapman) and author of *The Smart Stepfamily*

"When couples come for counseling, they are frequently explicit with their request: 'I need tools to build a stronger relationship.' *Relationship Essentials* responds to this request in a comprehensive way by providing ways to respectfully draw effective boundaries and other skills that are essential to the creation of meaningful relationships. Consider this book a practice manual for taking any or all of your relationships to a higher level."

— **Linda Bloom, LCSW**, coauthor of *101 Things I Wish I Knew When I Got Married*

"If there was ever a time when people were dying to feel known, seen, and heard, it is now. *Relationship Essentials* provides the tools that can lead people to healthy, rich relationships. Thank you, Lauren and Joneen, for this gift!"

— **Julie Baumgardner**, senior director of WinShape Marriage

"Relationships form the foundation of a meaningful, fulfilling life. *Relationship Essentials* is an extremely helpful guide to enhancing relationships and dramatically improving communication. It offers practical and effective methods to heal, deepen, and enrich relationships so that you can attain your highest quality of life."

— **Dan Willis**, police captain (ret.) and author of
*Bulletproof Spirit: The First Responder's Essential Resource
for Protecting and Healing Mind and Heart*

"*Relationship Essentials* is a wise and practical guide to living and working with others. It's a fun, easy read — yet amazingly comprehensive with tips and tools that range from difficult topics like conflict and boundaries to everyday habits like gratitude and respect."

— **Susan Campbell, PhD**, author of
Getting Real and *From Triggered to Tranquil*

"Strong, healthy, positive relationships are an important foundation of human flourishing. But cultivating such relationships takes wisdom and skill. *Relationship Essentials* offers practical guidance, delivered in an engaging and down-to-earth style, for developing the satisfying relationships necessary for a vibrant, generative life. Highly recommended!"

— **Matthew T. Lee**, director of empirical research at the
Harvard Human Flourishing Program

RELATIONSHIP ESSENTIALS

RELATIONSHIP ESSENTIALS

Skills to
**Feel Heard, Fight Fair,
and Set Boundaries**
in All Areas of Life

LAUREN REITSEMA
— and —
JONEEN MACKENZIE

New World Library
Novato, California

New World Library
14 Pamaron Way
Novato, California 94949

Text design by Tona Pearce Myers

Library of Congress Cataloging-in-Publication data is available.

Names: Reitsema, Lauren, author. | Mackenzie, Joneen, author.
Title: Relationship essentials : skills to feel heard, fight fair, and set boundaries in all areas of life / Lauren Reitsema and Joneen Mackenzie.
Description: Novato, CA : New World Library, [2021] | Includes bibliographical references. | Summary: "Illustrates ten research-backed methods for forming, maintaining, and improving healthy interpersonal relationships with friends, family, and coworkers"-- Provided by publisher.
Identifiers: LCCN 2021037311 | ISBN 9781608687619 (paperback) | ISBN 9781608687626 (epub)
Subjects: LCSH: Interpersonal relations--Research. | Social skills.
Classification: LCC HM1106 .R435 2021 | DDC 302--dc23
LC record available at https://lccn.loc.gov/2021037311

First printing, November 2021
ISBN 978-1-60868-761-9
Ebook ISBN 978-1-60868-762-6
Printed in Canada on 100% postconsumer-waste recycled paper

 New World Library is proud to be a Gold Certified Environmentally Responsible Publisher. Publisher certification awarded by Green Press Initiative.

10   9   8   7   6   5   4   3   2   1

For everyone who knows what it feels like to be isolated, alone, and longing to be known. Relationships can be challenging, but they are worth working for. May the tools in this book make building strong connections a little easier.

For our community of family and friends who have nurtured authentic relationships with us. Thank you for creating space to experience true belonging. We love you!

CONTENTS

INTRODUCTION

We are the granddaughter and daughter-in-law of an architect. He always said that with the proper tools, he could build anything. When it comes to homebuilding, crews follow a detailed blueprint and use a toolbox packed with supplies to make the architect's vision a reality. For building human relationships, most of us start without any blueprint or toolbox. Strong relationships are the foundation of life success, yet people are left to their own devices to build them. In navigating relationships we are often told to "follow your heart," but without a map and guideposts, this advice can often lead us astray. What if we approached a road trip with this same serendipitous plan —.just get behind the wheel and drive? Would we reach our destination?

Lauren: My first solo cross-country road trip took me from Denver to Dallas in a '97 Nissan Sentra. As I took the wheel, I pictured commercials of smiling people in aviator sunglasses with their windows rolled down, wind-blown hair, and rock ballads blasting from the speakers. These commercials often show a car — presumably one with much more appeal than my Sentra — on a winding road into the great unknown. I could not wait for this experience.

This drive took place before the days of GPS navigation and Siri, so my AAA road map sat beneath the steering wheel with my route highlighted in yellow. Heading out, I breezed through the first three songs burned onto my mix CD: "You Can Go Your Own Way," by Fleetwood Mac. Next, a Deadhead favorite, "Truckin'," and the Cochrane chorus of "Life Is a Highway." Then I glanced at my digital dashboard clock and noticed that twenty-two minutes had passed, and I was almost a third of the way through my soundtrack. Texas was still more than eleven hours away, yet I was already feeling the need for a stop. By the end of the trip, I realized that I am not someone who likes the journey. I much prefer the destination.

Have you ever considered what those car commercials do not show you? What about the research required to chart your course, or the financial planning needed to budget for gas and pay for hotels? Do the images on TV show the luggage you struggled to cram into your trunk or the police cars in the medians waiting to catch speeding drivers? Do they prepare us for flat tires, blizzards, or crawling through construction zones? For a successful road trip you need a plan, a road map, a reliable car, snacks, gas, and good company.

Healthy relationships, too, require a road map, but this information alone is not enough to change behavior: we need guided practice. With limitless information available on the internet, it might seem that we can teach ourselves everything we need to know. Information without application, however, falls short. Think about a surgeon. If someone made it through medical school, memorizing all the information from a textbook, but never put their knowledge into practice, they would never gain the skills necessary to perform life-saving surgery. If professional athletes watched videos of every previous championship team and spent hours studying playbooks without trying those plays on the field, they would never develop the skills and teamwork needed to win.

Like any other skill, managing human relationships requires knowledge, resources, and information, and each must be practiced and applied. What we learn about relationships is often gained solely through observation of other people. Unfortunately, the patterns we observe are not always healthy ones. This form of learning leaves generations vulnerable to repeating toxic cycles and robbing themselves of the experience of deep and loving relationships.

Relationship Essentials aims to fill that gap by providing tools and guidance for developing healthy connections. What an incredible journey it has been to create this book alongside my mom, Joneen Mackenzie, the founder of The Center for Relationship Education, an organization looking to disrupt the pattern of relationship discord and introduce a skills-based approach for helping people live connected lives.

The mission of The Center for Relationship Education is to provide relationship skills training to everyone. *Relationship Essentials* will equip you with ten proven tools for repairing, maintaining, and improving healthy connection and relationship satisfaction. As you read, we invite you to practice applying the tools in your everyday life. You do not need to understand every tool before you begin trying it out. The more you work with the tools, the more skills you will develop for building strong, supportive relationships. Note your favorites and keep each tool handy to use on any DIY relationship tune-ups.

THE THREE *C'S*
OF COMMUNICATION

TOOL: Power Drill — Enable powerful and complete connection by breaking communication down into three specific components: content, context, and connection. All three must work together like three interdependent components of a power drill.

We need to talk. Reading these words likely increases your heart rate and heightens your anxiety. Why? Because "We need to talk" is a phrase often interpreted as a signal of discord or strife. Talking, however, is the essence of connection. Healthy, clear communication is the foundation of successful relationships. Communication breakdown is common when we do not understand *how* to communicate. We often oversimplify the difficulties of communicating with others. A commonly offered remedy for miscommunication is "Just talk." Friends are leaving you out? Just talk. Your boss is treating you unfairly? Just talk. Your mom is embarrassing you? Just talk. But this advice minimizes the complexity and challenges of the communications process.

Building a relationship is one of the most important projects we face, yet most of us have few tools in our toolbox to help us. Each chapter of *Relationship Essentials* introduces you to one tool for achieving successful connections. The first is the Power Drill. It's a tool we often use to insert screws for connecting pieces of wood when framing a wall or putting together furniture. A task like this involves three components: the drill itself, the drill bit, and the screw. If any component is missing, we can't complete the task. In a similar way, communication involves three components: content (the drill), context (the bit), and connection (the screw). Below we examine each of these in depth.

Content

Here we define *content* as the substance of the message we want to communicate. Taking time to think about content sets the stage for connection. We are often advised, "Think before you speak." We suggest reframing this advice to "Think *about* what you speak." This rephrasing reminds us to choose carefully what we communicate. The following questions offer a guide for crafting meaningful content.

- What outcome are you trying to achieve by relaying your message?
- What words will provide the most clarity for the person with whom you are communicating?
- How much information do you need to provide to achieve your communication goal? Are you tempted to add or exaggerate information for the sake of drama?
- Is your message phrased in a way that would enable the other person to repeat it back to you accurately?

These questions can help us refine the content of our communications, selecting the information that is most relevant and important for others to know and expressing it in a way that helps them understand what we are asking for.

Sometimes communication breaks down because people feel stuck in silence. Have you ever been in a relationship situation where one or both parties won't communicate beyond "I have nothing to say" or "There is nothing to talk about"? These comments frequently indicate not an absence of issues or feelings in need of discussion, but a lack of relationship safety or a lack of desire to communicate.

Our brains are seething with thoughts and information. Rarely are we truly stuck with nothing to talk about. According to a study conducted at Stanford University, "The cerebral cortex [the outermost layer of the brain, and the site of many higher-order brain functions] alone has 125 trillion synapses. In another study, it was reported that 1 synapse can store 4.7 bits of information. Neurons are the cells which process and transmit messages within the brain, and synapses are the bridges between neurons which carry the transmitted messages. Running the numbers, the brain regularly engages 125 trillion synapses at 4.7 bits/synapse, and about 1 trillion bytes, equaling 1 TB (terabyte) [of information processing]." With this volume of processing going on in our brains, we would expect a wealth of unique thoughts. That said, we must not justify our stifled communication with the common excuse "I have nothing to say." Instead, it is important to learn to apply skills for discerning which of our thoughts merit sharing with others. We refer to this step in the communication process as *crafting content*.

Crafting content is like the task restaurant owners face when creating a menu. With limitless possible combinations of ingredients, owners must develop dishes that reflect their own unique style and then find the words to convey the essence of these creations. The best menu descriptions are specific (listing individual ingredients and describing flavors), accurate, and appealing. Communicating with another person is like preparing a signature dish for them: it honors your individual identity while also respecting the tastes and dietary preferences of the person to whom it is offered. Not everyone will enjoy every option on the menu. With this in mind, it is important that the offerings use appetizing ingredients and are presented with care. Like menu offerings, your messages will not always be what someone is eager to partake of. Do consider, however, trying to present your content in a way that does not leave the recipient feeling disgusted and sick. Be sure to plate your message tactfully and with consideration for the people seated around the table.

After crafting your message content, it is important to consider the second *C* in the communication process: context.

Context
Technology

Context is the medium through which content travels and the setting in which it is delivered. In today's world, the media most often utilized in communication channels are technology-based. There are millions of paths messages can take to arrive at their destinations. Phones enable text messages, emails, video-conference calls, chats, and social media exchanges. They also allow old-fashioned voice calls. Statements can be written electronically or in ink, spoken live, or recorded. Yet these advances in technological connection may not have enhanced our capacity for personal connection. Although it feels convenient and culturally normal to correspond almost exclusively through digital platforms, research affirms that this kind of communication fails to match the richness and efficiency of face-to-face interaction.

Lauren: I grew up on the cusp of the millennial generation. The first computer in our home was a boxy machine with a green rectangular cursor, famous for flashing over every letter typed on its keyboard. We had one video game called B.C.'s Quest in which a pixelated caveman rode along a path while we used a joystick to guide him away from falling rocks. Less than fifteen years after saving the princess from the caveman's attack, I had a Nokia cell phone in my pocket with more processing power than that computer. Technological advances have rapidly changed societal expectations. Today text message channels are considered fully appropriate for initiating, nurturing, and even ending relational pursuits.

If you are around teenagers, or are one yourself, you are likely familiar with the term *promposal*. This word (referring to the surprising ways people ask dates to a high school prom) was featured among Merriam-Webster's selection of new and popular "words we are watching" as potential dictionary additions. Because the prom is a rite of passage involving elaborate, creative, and costly preparations, I (Lauren) would never have believed that any teenager would accept a prom invitation via text message. Yet according to a survey of 1,155 teens by Text-Plus, a social texting app, 40 percent would ask a date to the prom via text, and 66 percent would accept a texted invitation.

This result suggests that society has made a dramatic shift away from face-to-face interactions to technology-mediated exchanges — not only among US high schoolers but among different generations and cultures across the globe. Technology makes communication possible when it otherwise might not be, but it does not enhance the experience. It omits the nonverbal cues necessary to accurately assess another person's tone, body language, and intent. A study titled "Can You

Connect with Me Now?" affirms that even the presence of a mobile phone or device decreases closeness, trust, and empathy between partners. Empirical evidence indicates that the mere presence of mobile phones during interactions inhibits the development of interpersonal closeness and trust and reduces the extent to which individuals feel empathy and understanding from their partners. These effects were most pronounced if individuals were discussing a personally meaningful topic.

Electronic communication may also lead to less favorable communication exchanges in business. In an article in the *Harvard Business Review*, Vanessa K. Bohns writes that in a business setting, "a face-to-face interaction is 34 times more successful than an email. ... [However,] participants who made requests over email felt essentially just as confident about the effectiveness of their requests as those who made their requests face-to-face." She advises that "if your office runs on email and text-based communication, it is worth considering whether you could be a more effective communicator by having conversations in person. It is often more convenient and comfortable to use text-based communication than to approach someone in-person, but if you overestimate the effectiveness of such media, you may regularly — and unknowingly — choose inferior means of influence."

What can we take from these findings about the effects of technology on communication? Simply being aware of the connection gaps caused by technology can remind us of the importance of trust, closeness, and empathy in communication. To help you develop awareness of how technology may affect your relationships, we have created a calendar that allows you to track your technology usage on a typical day. After finishing this exercise, commit to trying face-to-face communication as an alternative to technology, and see for yourself what a difference it can make.

TIME AND TECHNOLOGY WORKSHEET

Fill in the blanks below:

- I normally send or receive ___ text messages per day.
- I spend about ___ hours using social media per day.
- I am on my cell phone ___ minutes per day.
- I send ___ pictures per day from my cell phone.
- I normally watch ___ shows per day.
- I watch ___ movies per month at home and go to the movies ___ times per month.
- I spend ___ hours per day gaming on an electronic device.

In the schedule below, mark the hours when you use technology during your day.

Time Spent Using Technology

06:00 AM	03:30 PM
06:30 AM	04:00 PM
07:00 AM	04:30 PM
07:30 AM	05:00 PM
08:00 AM	05:30 PM
08:30 AM	06:00 PM
09:00 AM	06:30 PM
09:30 AM	07:00 PM
10:00 AM	07:30 PM
10:30 AM	08:00 PM
11:00 AM	08:30 PM
11:30 AM	09:00 PM
12:00 PM	09:30 PM
12:30 PM	10:00 PM
01:00 PM	10:30 PM
01:30 PM	11:00 PM
02:00 PM	11:30 PM
02:30 PM	12:00 AM
03:00 PM	12:30 AM

Setting

Another element of context is the setting or scene in which your message is communicated. When you're driving, to ensure a safe trip, it is important to know the road conditions. Similarly, when communicating, you need to consider the conditions in which your message is being sent and received. Are you trying to communicate your message in the middle of a deep fog when the receiver cannot see you coming? Are there noises and traffic lights impairing your focus? Are billboards distracting you from what you were trying to say? The setting of your communication is a vital component of successful communication. We don't always have control over the setting, and there is always the risk of unexpected roadblocks. Still, there are things we can do to clear the path for effective and productive communication.

1. **Limit distractions.** Turn off technology and mute excess noise. If others are around, choose a private setting where you won't be interrupted. Being physically present is not enough for respectful connection. Limiting distractions helps signal both physical and emotional presence.

2. **Designate conversation zones.** Whether in your home, your office, your school, or your neighborhood, earmark specific places that can become dedicated conversation zones. In these zones, set expectations around shutting down tech devices and agreeing to focus on face-to-face communication.

3. **Take a trip.** Not every meaningful conversation requires a fancy getaway, but studies show that a

simple change of scenery can increase attention and engagement. You do not have to go far. You might choose an outdoor pavilion for your staff meeting or a backyard firepit to reconnect with friends.

Connection

Sometimes, even with careful attention to content and context, the communication falls short. Successful communication requires the third C: connection. Even with the best intentions, there are instances when the content we attempt to express misses the mark. Our words collide, causing hurt, rather than connecting to cultivate understanding. To ensure your communication leads to connection but not collision, remember AAA:

Avoid unnecessary surprises
Ask for feedback
Affirm understanding

Avoid Unnecessary Surprises

We love seeing someone's joy upon receiving a thoughtful gift or surprise. Fun surprises are the best. Conversely, nothing feels quite as deflating as when the offering is tossed aside or received with shock and dismay. The difficulty is that the giver has very little control over the recipient's response. With communication, too, we lack control over how the recipient might connect with our intended message. We can minimize misconnection by preparing the recipient for what is coming. A friendly, fair warning helps avoid unwelcome surprises.

Lauren: I wish someone had given me fair warning to

avoid a few unpleasant surprises I remember. For instance, the time I was strolling through a department store while using a swim diaper on my baby. While holding my baby on my hip, I felt a warm liquid dribbling down my leg and discovered that swim diapers do not block leakage but simply catch solids. If I had known this ahead of time, it would have really helped. In the same vein, we are less likely to experience stress and anxiety when driving if our phone's satellite map warns us about a traffic jam or an accident ahead. With time to prepare for what is coming, we can muster the coping skills needed to respond. The same is true for communication. If difficult news is coming, it's helpful to prepare the recipient ahead of time. To enhance connection, anticipate your listener's reactions and prepare the way for communication. Here are some examples of ways to prepare a listener to hear something difficult:

- I don't want to alarm you, but I received some hard news at work today. Can I tell you about it?
- I want you to know I care about you, but my feelings are really hurt. Are you willing to talk about it?
- Before we present these numbers to our boss, I want to make space for an honest conversation with you. I am feeling nervous and need your help to determine a plan.

Even if the content is not easy to digest, giving the listener a chance to prepare helps avoid discouraging, and sometimes toxic, reactions.

Ask for Feedback

If you ever had walkie-talkies as children, you know that they are fun to play with only if both parties participate in the dialogue. If a top-secret message gets through to the receiving device and the receiver does not respond, the messenger shakes the toy to check its batteries or repeats the message incessantly, asking for a response. The same is true of our interpersonal relationships: it is not fun to talk to someone who does not respond. Enhance connection by soliciting feedback before, during, and possibly after the conversation. Here are some examples of how to do this:

> **Before message delivery:** After I share what I want to tell you, I am going to pause so that you have a chance to reflect on what I said.
>
> **During message delivery:** I have more to say, but before I move on, would you mind sharing what you heard me say, so that I know it landed as intended?
>
> **After message delivery:** I know that was a lot to process, but it is important to me to verify that you heard what I was trying to say. Can we set a time later this week to check back in about this topic?

Asking for appropriate feedback honors both participants' roles in the communication process as equal and important.

Affirm Understanding

The last *A* in the connection process is to affirm understanding. Unless we know that a message has been both sent and received, communication is incomplete. When we approach one another with the goal of mutual understanding (rather than of proving ourselves and protecting our egos), relationships flourish. We can cultivate understanding in relationships through empathy, which is defined as the ability to understand and share the feelings of another. According to the Greater

Good Science Center, a research institute that studies the psychology, sociology, and neuroscience of well-being, empathy is "a key ingredient of successful relationships because it helps us understand the perspectives, needs, and intentions of others." When those involved sincerely seek empathetic understanding, even the most strained relationships have a chance to rebuild.

Affirming understanding can take many forms. One of the best resources we recommend is the Speaker Listener Technique, from the book *Fighting* for *Your Marriage*, by Drs. Howard Markman, Scott Stanley, and Susan Blumberg. Putting these principles into action does not necessarily lead to agreement, but it does guarantee that the intended message is received and understood. This technique requires that two people agree to adopt the roles of speaker and listener and follow specific communication rules to ensure safe dialogue and mutual understanding in conversations where it matters. First, pick up some object (such as a remote control or pen) to symbolize "the floor" when using this technique.

The Speaker Listener Technique

- **Rules for the Speaker**
  - **Speak for yourself. Don't mind-read.** Mind-reading statements sound something like this: "You think you are so much better than me," or "I know you are never wrong, but…" Be sure to speak from your own perspective when taking the role of the speaker.
  - **Keep statements brief. Don't go on and on.** When you share too much information, the listener can feel flooded and miss the important points you are trying to communicate.

◦ **Stop to let the listener paraphrase.** Leave room for natural breaks in your conversation to allow the listener to repeat what they hear in their own words and validate understanding.

- **Rules for the Listener**

  ◦ **Paraphrase what you hear.** Repeat what you feel the speaker is saying in your own words.

  ◦ **Focus on the speaker's message. Don't rebut.** Rather than preparing your response, pay attention to what is being said. A warning sign that you are rebutting is thinking or saying, "Okay, but…"

- **Rules for Both**

  ◦ **The person with the floor is the speaker.** The focus is on the speaker's point of view until the roles are switched.

  ◦ **The speaker keeps the floor while the listener paraphrases.** The listener's only job is to summarize what they hear without taking the role of speaker away from the other person.

  ◦ **Both parties share the floor.** During the conversation, each person has numerous chances to be both the speaker and the listener, with the floor changing hands as many times as needed to establish a good flow. A good time to pass the floor is usually after the speaker has shared a couple of points — and has verified accuracy in the listener's paraphrase — so the listener can express their thoughts.

Using the Speaker Listener Technique can feel unnatural at first; however, it has been shown to bridge understanding gaps and ensure accurate message delivery. It is not a format that is intended to communicate about everyday things, but rather, a powerful technique for when you want to slow down and establish mutual understanding. One of the most important elements is paraphrasing, where the listener can show the speaker that the message has been received. Examples of paraphrase statements include:

- So, what I hear you saying is…
- It sounds like…
- From your perspective…
- Let me see if I heard you correctly. You feel…

Use these lead-ins as a resource when trying the technique the first few times. After some practice, paraphrasing often becomes a natural and organic step in your communication patterns and helps reduce misunderstanding. You can use this potent listening skill in conversation with anyone, apart from the structure of the Speaker Listener Technique.

TAKEAWAY TOOL SUMMARY

Effective connection happens when we skillfully engage all three *C*'s of communication: context, content, and connection. Consider these three *C*'s as a framework for communication in all types of relationships. First, develop clear and meaningful content. Next, consider the context in which your message is transmitted: both the medium through which your message is delivered and the setting in which it will land. Finally, validate connection with the intended receiver to ensure understanding.

The Relationship Essentials tool metaphor for these three principles is the Power Drill. For a power drill to function, you need the drill itself, the appropriate drill bit for the project, and the screw to connect the materials you are drilling. The next time you get advice to "just talk," try plugging in your Power Drill instead. Applying content, context, and connection to each one of your conversations spins the communication in the right direction.

2

GETTING TO KNOW ALL ABOUT YOU

TOOL: Flashlight — Shine a spotlight on others and learn to take a genuine interest in them.

To be known is a universal desire of the human heart. Neuroscientists have found that when people hear their name spoken out loud, their brain activity increases. The sitcom *Cheers*, a television series that aired in the 1980s and early 90s, famously spoke about a place "where everybody knows your name." This tagline, and the show's storyline about a group of people who had a safe place to gather, connect, and feel seen, attracted millions of viewers.

What does it take to be known? In this chapter, we will explore the Relationship Essentials Flashlight tool and the power of putting others in the limelight to develop relationships based on belonging and connection.

Joneen: Growing up in Brooklyn, New York, in an Italian-Jewish neighborhood, I had many eyes watching me. Everyone was into everyone else's business. After school, I remember lingering at Kelly Park and playing handball until the smell of garlic and onion lured me home for dinner. Often, I got lost in a heated stickball game, lost track of time, and had to run home to make curfew. I can still hear all the women leaning out of their second- and third-story windows screaming, "It's time to get home!" as I sprinted down the street. When I was little, I found this annoying, but now I recognize the gift of a gaggle of community members watching out for me. My maternal grandparents lived in Manhattan and worked in the textile industry, my grandmother as a seamstress and grandfather as a cutter. My brother and I, aged eight and seven, took the subway and two buses by ourselves to my grandparents' apartment. Can you imagine? How the world has changed. My cousin, Marion, who worked in the beauty salon at Saks Fifth Avenue, helped nurture my love affair with Broadway shows. Through her vast network of New York personalities, she could get us behind the scenes at theaters.

Lauren: This big-city backdrop was extremely different from my upbringing in a quaint mountain town. I used to imagine what it was like for Mom to ride the subway and sit in the crowd at Radio City Music Hall or attend the Macy's Thanksgiving Day parade. As a child, I dreamed about visiting New York City, and for my thirteenth birthday, Mom made this dream a reality.

The city captivated me, with underground subway turnstiles, salty street-cart pretzels, and glittering marquee lights. The biggest thrill was seeing Broadway, because I was involved in musical theater. To this day, I can't always remember where I put my car keys, but I have a memory packed with a full repertoire of songs from musicals! One such tune is "Getting to Know You" from Rodgers and Hammerstein's *The King and I*. If you know it, go ahead and sing it with me.

The King and I is about the relationship between the king of Siam and Anna, a young English schoolteacher who travels to Siam to become governess to his children in the mid-nineteenth century. The musical ran on Broadway for nearly three years, and it has had many tours and revivals. It focuses on the developing love story between the Anna and the king. "Getting to Know You," sung by Anna when she first meets her new charges, is one of the most important songs in the show, because it alludes to building bridges across social and cultural divides. According to the musical's director, Barlette Sher, "The pure effort of that, the 'getting to know you' quality, is so impressive, now in our so deeply divided current country and world, in so many ways." Sher goes on to explain that sometimes the simple gesture of leaving your own cultural comfort zone, with a willingness to learn about someone else's, is the difference maker in narrowing the divide. Making the effort to know someone authentically, and feeling known by others, can help us break through biases and stereotypes and see individuals through an empathetic lens.

In a world where media and marketing reinforce the focus on self, learning to focus on others is key to forming and sustaining lasting, meaningful relationships. Putting others first and taking a genuine interest in their perspectives does not always come naturally. Self-care and self-awareness are important, but we must also cultivate and express our care and concern for others. Applying tools that help you focus on others, instead of yourself, will make your relationships closer and more satisfying for all.

Being Interested Makes You Interesting

Joneen: While raising my family, I was fascinated by, and intellectually curious about, the art of parenting. My shelves were lined with books on teaching children to consider others' interests and needs when they are hard-wired to put themselves first. One effective tactic is using play to help children develop social and emotional skills.

To demonstrate the value of putting others first, I developed a simple game with my toddlers. I sat on the floor opposite my children with my legs forming a V and asked each child to mimic my position. Next, I rolled a ball toward one of them. Whoever received the ball caught it between their legs and rolled it back to me, squealing with delight. This went on for several rounds, until I withheld the ball. The children would plead for me to roll it back to them. When I did not, they became frustrated, lost interest in the game, and stopped engaging with me. To mitigate their frustrations, I made it my goal to give them the last roll.

I continued this purposeful game throughout their elementary years, now throwing the ball rather than rolling it. When my kids entered adolescence, they sometimes asserted their independence by not engaging in conversation with me. I reminded them of the ball game and drew a parallel between their long-ago frustration at not receiving the ball and mine when they refused to engage in conversation. It worked: they remembered their frustration and reengaged with me.

This game illustrates the importance of other-centered communication. When we hog the ball, or refuse to roll it to others at all, we lose an opportunity for connection, leaving another person feeling isolated, frustrated, and disconnected. Keeping the ball to ourselves may feel good, but we must let go of it and roll it to others to engage in genuine connection.

One way to connect with others is by asking questions. According to one article on the topic, "Research has found people who are inquisitive are generally judged to be more intelligent and engaged." People who are interested are interesting.

Stay Open-Minded about Who You Invite to Play

We naturally connect with others who share similar interests, thoughts, and values. Aiming to avoid conflict, or to feel justified and right in our perspectives, we often form homogeneous social groups and develop few tools for connecting with individuals with differing backgrounds and beliefs. Additionally, our brains are wired to form first impressions of new acquaintances based on incomplete knowledge and biases, meaning that those impressions are often inaccurate.

Lauren: I enrolled in an interpersonal communications class during my freshman year of college. Most of the students enrolled were sophomores and juniors. The professor opened her lecture with "Welcome to Interpersonal Communications, section 205. This course is intended for sophomore-level enrollment and above. Are there any freshmen present today?" Like an elementary-school student eager to share the answer to a question, I shot up my hand. My confidence quickly ebbed as I saw that my hand was the only one raised.

After class, another student approached me and whispered, "Hey, I'm Ashley. Just so you know, I'm a freshman too." Initially I was angry, thinking, *Why didn't you help me out back there and raise your hand, too?* Next I felt relieved that I was not going to be the only freshman in the class, maybe struggling to keep up while learning the ropes of college. Finally, I was judgmental, tagging Ashley with all the stereotypes I had been fed in my Colorado upbringing about women from Texas with big hair and showy jewelry. The only thing I knew I had in common with Ashley was being a freshman in the class. Nothing about her seemed in alignment with my interests. I had instantly tagged her as someone I would never relate to, never understand, and never call a close friend.

Thankfully, my snap judgments were refuted as we spent more time together. Ashley became a roommate, and to this day she is one of my closest confidants.

Without leaving space for discovery with people we dismiss or judge, we miss opportunities for meaningful connections. Employing the Flashlight tool from the Relationship Essentials toolbox will enable you to practice and experience the benefits of other-centered communication.

Three Steps for Using the Flashlight

Picture yourself at an office party, a family gathering, or a hangout with friends. How do you feel as you visualize the scene?

- Are you enjoying pleasant conversation?
- Do you find yourself inspired by other people's creative ideas?
- Are you feeling safe and secure enough to show up as your authentic self?

If you answered no to any of these questions, you are not alone. Social settings can trigger anxiety, raising our heart rate and sometimes even causing sleepless nights beforehand. Anticipating conflict-ridden topics, we practice our rebuttals, research statistics defending our position, or simply avoid conversation with strangers altogether. Some people may engage with new acquaintances only if they are aided by an adult beverage. But conversation doesn't have to be a minefield. By using the Flashlight tool to illuminate people's particular interests and personality, you demonstrate graciousness and kindness rather than pride and ego. People who demonstrate these characteristics enjoy more positive interactions and are more esteemed and respected than those focused on touting themselves. Mastering thoughtful, open-ended questioning will help you make stronger connections, not only during potentially intimidating social scenarios but in all your relationships.

1. Ask Masterful Questions

Follow these guidelines when developing questions you can use to engage others in meaningful dialogue:

Stay Open-Ended

Open-ended questions are those that invite a response more nuanced than a simple yes or no. They give the respondent the opportunity to reveal details that go deeper than a short factual statement, which can halt conversation. Formulating open-ended questions requires preparation and focus. In exchanges with family and friends, we often limit our questions to factual inquiries, such as "How was your day?" and "What should we have for dinner?"

These questions are not bad questions — they do express interest. However, their structure invites only brief, predictable responses, like "Fine" or "Food." We get stuck in routine, patterned expressions, which limit the opportunity to deepen intimacy and spark interest. To make the conversation richer, try making your open-ended questions *specific* and *personal* to the individual you're talking to.

The table below lists familiar, conventional questions on the left and reformulated, open-ended versions of the questions on the right.

How was your day at work (or at school)?	What was something that happened during a meeting/class that made you feel valued as part of the team/group?
What's the weather like right now?	Does this weather bring back any memories for you?
Did you have a good week?	Looking back on the week, what is one moment that surprised you?
What should we have for dinner?	If we had a private chef, what would be on the menu?
How are you?	On a scale of one to ten, how's your mood, and why?

Asking personal, specific questions brings opportunities to learn more about the people in your life, and your demonstrated interest in them will in turn increase their curiosity and desire to engage with you.

Ask about Who People Are, Not about What They Do

Lauren: Whether we're conversing with someone we have known for years or a perfect stranger, we tend to ask the same, routine questions about work or school. Almost daily, when my husband and I return from our respective offices, the first words out of our mouths are "Welcome home. How was work?" Can you relate? This question typically engenders a one-word response, like "Stressful," "Tiring," "Okay," or "Fun."

There is nothing inherently wrong (or negative) in asking about work and school; we spend many of our waking hours in these settings, and what happens there is important. But these topics should not dominate our conversation.

I love watching teenagers make the transition between high school and higher education. It can be a difficult time, however, because they are bombarded by questions from parents, coaches, teachers, and friends: "So, where are you going to college? What do you plan to study next year? What career do you have in mind?" Although these questions have merit, they send the message that people are interested only in what you do with your life, not in who you are. In the same vein, when adults find themselves answering a barrage of questions about their work, they begin to understand their value as being rooted in their workplace accomplishments or financial success, which detracts from relationship satisfaction. When researcher Jessie Sun set out to test the quality of connection and social interaction, she discovered that "people do feel more socially connected when they are having self-disclosing or deeper conversations."

Small-talk, surface-level conversations often seem to suffice. But a growing body of social science research is now affirming that the quality of conversation affects the quality of connection. People feel valued, seen, and inspired by those who inquire not just about what they do but about who they are. If you engage people in conversation that goes beyond their work or studies, you will experience better relationship satisfaction.

Be Creative

When we think about the word *creative*, we often envision an artist, a musician, or a dancer. By definition, *creative* means "relating to or involving the imagination or original ideas, especially in the production of an artistic work." Creativity, however, is not limited to artistic fields: it is a quality everyone can engage in that helps us grow in every aspect of life. Learning to be creative in asking questions can enhance all relationships.

If creativity does not come naturally to you, consider using a resource designed to help. Many tools on the market can help spark thoughtful dialogue with others. Two of our favorites are *The If... Questions for the Game of Life* book series, and Table Topics cubes. Asking imaginative questions makes your interactions both more personal and more memorable. Make it your goal to have the person you are engaging think, *What a thoughtful and fun question! No one has ever asked me that before.*

Using these three principles of crafting questions, try reframing these common, bland questions into more creative, engaging ones.

What did you do today?
How are you?
What are your goals for this year?

The Flashlight tool uses masterful questions to enrich relationships, but it draws its power from two additional components, which you can remember with the help of the acronym AA (like the battery):

Affirm answers
Away from self

2. Affirm Answers

Asking a question is only part of a healthy dialogue. How you respond when a person answers your question is equally important. We can divide typical answers to conversational questions into four categories: *dismissing, minimizing, redirecting,* and *affirming.*

Dismissing is defined as "deciding that something or someone is not important and not worth considering" — in other words, ignoring or invalidating someone's response. Dismissal can be verbal or nonverbal. A verbal dismissal might take the form of a put-down: "You have no idea what you are talking about" or "That's a dumb idea." Nonverbal dismissal could take the form of walking away after the person answers, appearing distracted, ignoring the answer, or giving the person the silent treatment.

Minimizing behavior acknowledges the answer but characterizes its content as unimportant or invalid: for example, "You shouldn't feel that way" or "You're overreacting."

Redirecting involves the questioner taking the respondent's answer and steering it back to serve their own goal: "That's great, but in my experience..." or "Let's get back to what I was saying." Redirecting can also occur nonverbally, by simply ignoring the person or withholding a response.

The fourth type of response, *affirming,* is the type that signals appropriate use of the Flashlight tool. An affirming response acknowledges what is said and validates it as worthy. This does not always mean that you agree; rather, it demonstrates that you honor that person's perspective and their unique passions and convictions. "That's a really fascinating perspective" and "I can tell this topic is one that lights up your heart" are both examples of affirming speech. Affirming another's opinions allows space for mutual respect and edification. It makes you someone who is appreciated and trusted.

3. Steer Conversation Away from Yourself

The second *A* in the AA acronym, "away from self," is also vital to deepening relationships.

Joneen: Years ago, my husband refinanced a home belonging to two venture capitalists — a power-couple entrepreneurial team. They were so appreciative of the service they received that they insisted on taking us out to a five-star restaurant to thank him. The dinner went on for several courses and several hours. When we arrived home, I said to my husband, "Please never do that to me again!" The dinner was delicious, but the conversation was excruciating.

This couple's intent was good. They hoped to connect with us and express gratitude for my husband's services. But all they did was talk about themselves. During the entire meal, they did not ask us one question about ourselves. I had been excited about the event, anticipating great conversation and the chance to learn from their gutsy and creative careers. But the experience turned out to be less than affirming.

I do not fault this couple for the pattern of their conversation. In retrospect, it serves as a tangible example of habits that all of us are susceptible to. In *How to Win Friends and Influence People*, Dale Carnegie states, "When we are not engaged in thinking about some definite problem, we usually spend about 95 percent of our time thinking about ourselves." We start with a major impediment in learning to put others first. If only 5 percent of our thoughts are focused on others, we must exercise our brains to intentionally engage other-minded thinking. It may be an uphill climb, but it is always worth the effort.

Like any new skill, other-minded thinking requires practice. The "Not I" exercise below offers a fun and informative way to develop your "Away from self" discipline. We invite you to try it with family members and friends.

The objective of the exercise is to talk only about yourself, for two solid minutes, without using the word *I*. In our in-person training sessions, we place participants into pairs. Each person has two minutes to speak. The other person holds a plastic squeaky toy. Every time the speaker slips up and uses *I*, their partner squeezes the toy. No one ever wants to get "squeaked," but the room is always filled with the sound of squeaking and laughter. With heightened awareness and intentions, people get better at avoiding *I*.

As everyone regroups for discussion, we explore two questions:

- What makes this exercise challenging?
- What strategies did you employ to avoid saying *I*?

Responses to the first question include:

- We are so used to talking about ourselves, and we say *I* a lot more than we consciously realize.
- It's unnatural to talk about ourselves without saying *I*.

Responses to the second question include:

- We had to focus.
- We had to be intentional and thoughtful about our speech.
- We had to slow down and be creative.

The exercise illustrates how much our focus on self dominates our conversation. Once we become aware of this habit, we are better able to shift our thinking to focus on others. Although it may seem more natural and more fulfilling to talk about yourself in relationships, focusing on others has been shown to increase contentment. Michael McGee, a Stanford Medical School graduate and psychiatrist with over thirty years' experience in addiction recovery, writes, "Putting others first is a form of enlightened self-concern. It is in our best interest to do so, because living to love others is far more fulfilling than living to gratify ourselves. Just look carefully at your own life experience to see that this is true. Many of us experience this for the first time when we have children. In putting our children first, we experience the truth that putting others first is best for us. When we extend this practice to everyone in our lives, we realize great fulfillment."

Our society emphasizes self-focus and self-care. Although the idea of self-care stems from good intentions, constant self-focus can unintentionally harm relationships and reduce contentment. Adopting an other-minded approach benefits ourselves as well as other people.

TAKEAWAY TOOL SUMMARY

Engaging your Relationship Essentials Flashlight helps you place the spotlight on others, identifying you as someone who takes a genuine interest in other people and is perceived as intelligent and engaging.

Using the Flashlight involves:

1. Asking masterful questions
2. Affirming the respondent's answers
3. Steering your conversation away from yourself

Keep this tool in your relationship toolbox as a resource for truly getting to know those in your relationship circles.

3

ENOUGH IS ENOUGH

Why Boundaries Are Kind

 TOOL: Tape Measure — Learn to measure and mark your personal boundaries.

Creating boundaries in our relationships is not only kind but essential. All of us secretly know when we can push the limits and with whom we can push them. A student who behaves well with their regular teacher will sometimes act out and clown around when a substitute teacher takes over in a classroom. A child may push all the limits with a friend but toe the line when parents are present. An office supervisor who doesn't require accountability may end up with a team that is rudderless and unproductive. Boundaries do not restrict freedom: they enhance it. This chapter introduces the Relationship Essentials Tape Measure tool to help you establish and maintain healthy relationship boundaries.

Joneen: Everyone who has celebrated a birthday around me has seen my traveling party in a bag. This black, canvas tote contains everything I need to stage an impromptu celebration, complete with backdrop banner, party hat, inflatable triple layer cake, and boom box that plays "Happy Birthday to You." For decades I've toted this bag everywhere I go in case a friend, family member, or stranger happens to have a birthday. I love to celebrate people. Everyone deserves a party to celebrate another 365 days around the sun. This mindset carries over to weddings, work promotions, baby showers, and holiday festivities. Name something to celebrate, and I can produce a celebration.

When I was raising my four children, we lived in the foothills of Colorado's Rocky Mountains, with views of snow-capped peaks and wildflower meadows. Herds of elk bugled outside our kitchen window in the morning, and porcupines squealed beneath our deck. We discovered the porcupines during a deck remodeling project we began one June. The construction was scheduled to finish well in advance of our annual July 4 barbecue, but as so often happens with construction projects, the crew was running behind.

Everything was finished except for the railings. Several neighbors and friends were scheduled to join us for burgers and a make-your-own ice cream sundae bar. I put the finishing touches on the serving platters and called the kids outside. They joined me on the deck but stopped just inches from the back door, palpably anxious and hesitant about being outside. Although the deck had plenty of safe space away from the edges, they felt unsafe without the railings in place. I realized we would need to postpone our celebration until the deck was finished.

Measure Your Limits

My kids are not the only ones who have experienced anxiety in the absence of clearly defined boundaries. Years ago, an educational researcher set out to evaluate the behavior of schoolchildren during an outdoor expansion project. Education students at a nearby university asked the contractor not to complete the fence around the playground. Researchers observed the behavior of the children (ages 5–11) during recess. All the children, without exception, chose to play close to the school building. Months later, when the fence was erected, they ran and played freely on the entire playground; kids even buried their little noses in the fence. This study demonstrates the freedom that comes with established limits.

A tape measure is helpful in measuring and marking boundaries in construction projects. In relationships, it can be a metaphor for defining your personal boundaries. We draw different boundaries for different types of relationships. We have defined four categories of boundaries or limits that you can remember with the acronym *TAPE*:

Time limits: How much time are you willing to commit to different relationships?

Auditory limits: What are you willing to listen to?

Physical limits: How do you define your personal space? Who is allowed to access it, and in what ways?

Emotional limits: How do you establish emotional safety in relationships?

Time Limits

Lauren: Sometimes an outside perspective is required to help us see things in our actions or behaviors that we fail to recognize in ourselves. A colleague recently remarked that "Lauren is the only person I know who schedules her day to the minute."

"Really?" I responded. "I consider myself to be unscheduled and spontaneous!" Apparently my self-awareness lens was blurred, because everyone laughed. Reflecting on this incident, I realized that I calculate time to the minute when chairing meetings, running errands, or grabbing a snack. I guess it is not the norm to report your estimated time of arrival as 9:07 a.m.? As my colleague lovingly pointed out, I am rigid about budgeting and spending my time. This is not because I have a militaristic mindset but because I honor time limits as a relational boundary. Time is a limited human commodity. To be able to offer our time generously in significant relationships, we must be intentional and disciplined about how we use it.

Think about the following scenarios:

- You call a friend at 8:30 a.m. during your commute. With an important meeting scheduled to start at 9:00 a.m., you assume you have plenty of time to get off the call and be punctual for the meeting. The conversation, however, goes much longer than expected, and you anxiously await a break in your friend's speech to bring the call to a close, so that you don't walk into the meeting still talking on the phone.

- You agree to join friends for a game night, planning to get home at a reasonable hour to rest and prep for a speaking event the following day. But tie-breaking rounds of the game keep you playing much later than you intended. You wake up late and arrive for your presentation with a foggy brain.

- You are looking forward to a long-overdue date night with your partner. The babysitter is a close family friend who often seeks your advice. When she arrives, she asks for a minute of your time to get a quick piece of advice and proceeds to recount a delicate personal situation that leaves you feeling guilty about ignoring her. Listening to her delays your romantic evening plans by half an hour.
- You have had many conversations with your children about the importance of getting up when their alarm clock sounds, yet their persistent use of the snooze feature still turns mornings into a stressful whirlwind.

How would you describe the people who seem to cause these disruptions and delays in your schedule? We often cast them as *rude, inconsiderate, disrespectful,* or *selfish.* However, it is unfair to blame anyone but ourselves if incidents like this become regular occurrences. Each of these examples is a way we allow others to break our personal time boundaries.

To avoid time-limit breakers in your relationships:

1. Include time in your schedule to allow for delays.
2. Schedule things to the nearest ten minutes rather than the nearest minute.
3. Be clear about the limits on your time: for example, at an evening meeting, you might say, "I'm so thankful I get time with you tonight. I wanted to let you know I made a commitment to read my daughter a story at eight o'clock, so I'll have to leave at 7:45."
4. Be fully present during the time you designate for

interpersonal connection. Turn off phones, ask open-ended questions, and have a plan for enjoying and engaging in activities together.

Setting and honoring time limits can help maximize your relationship satisfaction.

Auditory Limits

If you have children, or spend time around children, you've likely said more than once, "I don't want to hear it anymore!" One thing that often provokes this remark is tattling among siblings: "He drew a mustache on my art project!" "She ate a piece of my candy!" "He coughed on my dolls!" "She wore my shoes without asking!" Just writing these examples makes us want to stop typing and shout, "Enough! I don't want to hear it anymore!" Although we don't often think about it explicitly, it's important to define what we are willing to listen to from others. By refusing to listen to tattling, we make it clear that we will not tolerate children's attempts to shift blame and punishment onto one another, and we convey to them that they must work the problem out on their own.

The concept of auditory limits applies to all types of relationships. Consider your core values and what types of conversation or language dishonor these values. For example, if you are an animal rights activist, yet your friends constantly brag about hunting victories, these conversations may violate your auditory limits. If you have been hurt after learning that a trusted friend said negative things about you behind your back, but you listen to gossip from others, that gossip breaks your auditory boundaries. Setting limits on what you will and will not listen to in relationships can save you from conflict and discord.

Auditory limits come in many forms. For example, in your home or workplace you may choose not to tolerate the following:

- explicit language
- bigoted speech
- hurtful gossip
- self-deprecating, critical speech
- constant pessimism and negativity

Setting auditory limits does not mean refusing to listen to different opinions and perspectives. Everyone has the right to enjoy and express their own opinions and thoughts, but when conflicting thoughts and opinions freely circulate without boundaries, relationships often suffer. As you become proficient about measuring and communicating your auditory limits, people will learn to respect them. For example, we come from a long lineage of family members who served (or currently serve) in the US military. This upbringing molded a strong sense of honor toward those in military roles. Understanding their sacrifice firsthand enhances the patriotism we feel for our country. Negative discourse about military funding or policy affects us more, and more personally, than it might affect others without familial military experience. This example helps communicate the value of setting boundaries around what you are willing to listen to. Knowing how we feel about this issue helps set and communicate the boundary line. Saying something like, "Please refrain from criticizing military institutions when you're with me. It changes my mood for the worse, and I don't want to be in that mindset while we are together."

What is your version of "military"? It is important to

establish healthy communication around these types of topics in your relationships, defining and articulating your own auditory limits and respecting those of others. A sign of maturity in relationships is being able to choose not to push another person's buttons and boundaries just to get a rise out of them. People will not always agree with your position and worldview, but we can appreciate and honor differences without breaking boundaries for the sake of defending our egos or stirring up drama.

Setting auditory limits may feel nerve-racking at first, but it decreases the probability of experiencing anger and stress when you are with others who have differing opinions.

Physical Limits

Have you ever noticed social behavior patterns in a self-seating restaurant or bar? In Western culture, we naturally choose tables that are spaced apart from one another, and, unless the room is crowded, we are put off by a stranger coming and sitting right next to us. We have instinctive notions of personal space that prompt us step back when others come too close. As we get to know and trust a person, we begin to feel more comfortable reducing the space between us. Physical space preferences are not universal; they vary with country and culture. Regardless of your background, however, physical limits are an important part of healthy relationships.

Physical limits in personal relationships can be difficult to define. The following exercise can help teach this social-emotional skill. If you are reading with someone else, go ahead and try this with us. (Be sure you know this person, or you risk crossing one another's physical boundaries with the exercise itself!)

Stand up and face one another with your arms outstretched and fingertips close enough to touch. We call this distance *acquaintance space*. Next, bend your arms ninety degrees and step forward so that your palms are almost touching. We call this *friendship space*. Finally, place the palms of your hands on your own shoulders and step forward so that your elbows are almost touching the other person's. We call this *intimate space*. Depending on the nature of your relationship, you and your partner may have felt uncomfortable in one another's intimate space. This is a good sign: it shows awareness of physical limits.

Lauren: When I was in college, I had the opportunity to study abroad to fulfill the requirements of my Spanish minor. After an eight-week immersion course in Cádiz, Spain, my roommate and I took advantage of the Eurail Pass, which offers discounted train travel to students, and traveled to Italy, Germany, and Switzerland. Since this was our first international travel adventure, we expected language barriers and missteps along the route. Thankfully, we encountered fewer than we expected, until we took an overnight train from Florence to Munich, with bunks reserved in a sleeping compartment. Boarding the train, we followed the train conductor to our compartment. He did not speak English but stared at our tickets with a disgruntled expression on his face. Something was obviously wrong. We arrived at the compartment with the number matching our ticket, but the conductor refused to let us in, shaking his head to indicate that there was no room. Frustrated and tired, I pointed to the number on our ticket. When he refused to open the door, I jostled the handle myself. It opened, and we found that the compartment was already occupied by a family of four from Germany. After a lot of hand gesturing and negotiating, using my best version of charades, we convinced the reluctant family to let us use the unoccupied top two bunks, just inches from the ceiling.

Embarrassed, we crawled into our bunks, hoping this major personal space violation would soon become a distant memory. The next morning, in the sunlight, we stared sheepishly across the three-foot aisle, locking eyes with the travelers who had shared their private sleeper cabin with two American tourists. There was no escaping the shame and discomfort: we averted our gaze as we ate boiled eggs and croissants. As it turned out, our sleeper car number was correct, but our tickets were for the wrong date. The emotion I felt at this violation of other people's physical boundaries forever reminds me of the importance of physical limits in relationships.

My experience was merely embarrassing, but violating physical limits can have much more serious consequences. Violating physical limits with colleagues may lead to HR proceedings and job termination. Crossing physical boundaries in a romantic relationship may leave one or both partners as victims of assault. Refusing to honor these boundaries with friends may signal disrespect or violate trust. Safeguard your relationships by outlining physical limits that are clearly understood by all parties.

Answer these questions to help define physical limits in your relationships:

- Are you a hugger? If so, when and how often are hugs appropriate?
- How close is too close for you when communicating with a stranger?
- In romantic relationships, what level of physical intimacy is desired and appropriate for you and your partner?

- Who in your life has permission to occupy:
  - acquaintance space?
  - friendship space?
  - intimate space?

Emotional Limits

Joneen: My 90-year-old mom epitomizes every Italian stereo-type in the kitchen. From the moment her feet touch the floor in the morning, she thinks about what she is going to serve for breakfast, lunch, and dinner, and guests are always welcome and expected around her table. When she comes to Colorado to visit, she takes on the role of chef. Sitting next to me at the table, she asks, "Would you like more?," to which I usually re-spond, "No thanks, I'm stuffed." She then immediately serves me another helping. *Did she not hear me? Is overserving guests an Italian tradition? Is eating well so important to her that she simply ignores my requests?* Thinking about each one of these questions and taking into account her age, her habits, and her intentions, I choose not to rebuke her and hurt her feelings; however, this behavior violates my emotional boundaries.

Honoring emotional boundaries means separating your feelings from someone else's, understanding how transparent you are willing to be with others, and respecting the emotional process of the other person. When you talk about something that means a lot to you, if the listener responds positively and signals that they would like to know more, you share more. If the listener is indifferent or even harsh, you know it is not safe to share, and you avoid becoming closer to this person. We all know someone who overshares intimate details of their lives and feelings. It is awkward for the listener and clumsy for the speaker. Emotional limits are commonly misunderstood and often violated.

Suppose you arrive home from a crazy workday, and your partner is extremely excited about a project they have just completed. As soon as you walk into the house, they meet you in the entryway and grab your hand to show off their work. You ask whether you could get the tour after a few hours of recovery and rest. If your request is met with resistance, your partner may grumble about your lack of interest and attention, while you stew in exhaustion and frustration. This kind of mismatch of feelings is a common result of breaking emotional boundaries. Violations are often subtle. One of you feels angry, the other annoyed.

Sometimes it is hard to recognize or name these feelings, so here are some signs that might indicate a violation of emotional boundaries:

- internal or external frustration
- a feeling of walking on eggshells
- resentment
- anxiety
- increased stress
- feeling incompetent
- feeling selfish
- guilt
- fear

Another red flag is controlling behavior. When someone makes decisions for you, or tells you what you should do, when you should do it, and how you should do it, that is a possible violation of your emotional boundaries.

To set emotional limits, you need to feel good about yourself. Something Lauren often says is: "If you view yourself as high-hanging fruit, someone who wants to be in relationship with you needs to put energy in and work for it. If you view yourself as low-hanging fruit, people can take you for granted and just pick you off the ground without contributing any effort." When you lack self-confidence, you are liable to take on other people's moods and feelings, which is unhealthy and unsatisfying in relationships. Modeling healthy emotional boundaries is a way to establish fruitful connections.

You cannot force another person to be the way you want them to be, and others cannot mold you into who they want you to be. Take responsibility for your emotional health and allow people to do the same. Let us replay the scenario above, of returning from work, with new awareness of emotional limits. Instead of greeting you in the entryway, your partner waits for you to settle in and offers you some breathing space. Once you have decompressed, the partner says, "I am so excited about what I accomplished today. When would be a good time to share it with you?" This gesture demonstrates excitement while honoring your need to decompress before engaging emotionally.

Establishing healthy emotional boundaries is necessary for forging healthy connections. We will expand on strategies for establishing emotional safety in a later chapter. In the context of boundary setting, acknowledge your emotions and work to preserve a distinction between your emotional experience and that of others.

Broken Boundaries

You have likely experienced the shock that follows when a tape measure's lock is accidentally released. The sharp-edged metal tape springs back into its case, often slicing a finger or pinching your skin. This startles us, and it hurts! The same thing happens when we experience broken boundaries in our relationships. Yet there is always an opportunity to measure again. It is never too late to establish healthy boundaries, and every type of relationship benefits from them.

In construction and carpentry, the rule is to measure first, not to dive into the project and then measure. The same is true when you apply TAPE to your relationships. Determine your boundaries ahead of time to increase the probability that your boundaries will be honored in personal interactions.

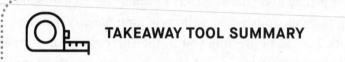

TAKEAWAY TOOL SUMMARY

Boundaries are often viewed as restrictive. However, when navigating relationships, the opposite is true: setting and keeping boundaries enhances our sense of freedom and trust. Practice the skills of measuring your TAPE and marking your boundaries through clear and consistent communication.

4

TELL ME
WHAT YOU WANT

TOOL: Adjustable Wrench — Establish the nuts and bolts of your expectations, and widen or narrow your grip when identifying the disappointment of an expectation gap.

Everyone has expectations. They are commonly understood as needs, wants, or desires, both short-term and long-term. Unmet expectations play a big role in our frustrations, hurts, and disappointments. Learning to better understand the power of expectations, particularly in our relationships, is critical. The Relationship Essentials Adjustable Wrench will help you define and adjust your expectations to maintain a tighter grip on relationship satisfaction.

Lauren: In a previous chapter, we described Joneen's love of birthday celebrations. She believes life is precious, so people deserve to feel valued and special by celebrating the day they were born. While Mom totes her famous traveling party bag, I put a different spin on birthday tradition. My secret weapon is a pre–birthday party interview to learn the expectations of the birthday person. A few years ago, my oldest daughter, Lia, was approaching her fifth birthday. In keeping with our tradition, I arranged a mother-daughter ice cream outing to talk about her birthday wishes. Pen and paper in hand, I asked her about her vision for the perfect party. "Go ahead, honey," I said. "Tell me what you are thinking for your birthday this year."

"Mom," Lia started in, "may I please have an Elsa party?" Like many girls of her age, she was enchanted with the recently released Disney movie *Frozen*, and she began to communicate her vision for an ice-princess extravaganza.

"That sounds amazing," I replied. "What do you have in mind?" *Frozen*-themed party supplies were available from any party store, and costumes were just one click away online. *This will be a cakewalk*, I thought to myself.

Her blue eyes widened, and the pitch of her voice rose.

"If it's okay, I'd like to build an ice castle in the yard. It would be awesome to have Anna and Elsa fly in from Arendelle to sing 'Let It Go' with my friends. After that, we can have a snowball fight with Olaf [the magical snowman Elsa and Anna built as children in their castle]. Then, cake and presents. Sound good?"

As I digested my daughter's request, the only thing frozen was my mind. My plan to make her birthday wish come true had just hit a major roadblock. I knew Lia had a creative spirit and a zest for imaginative play, but I had failed to consider the implications of inviting her to create expectations that only Disney's team of special-effects experts could fulfill. Leaving aside the challenges of having flying characters arrive on the scene, Lia's birthday is in May, precluding any possibility of creating an ice castle. Although my daughter had clearly communicated her expectations, I lacked the capacity to meet them. Without adjusting those expectations, I was sure to have a very disappointed birthday girl.

Rather than squelch her dream completely, I engaged the Relationship Essentials Adjustable Wrench tool and thought about my options for decreasing the expectation gap. After we discuss the nuts and bolts of expectations in relationships, we will revisit this story and show how applying this tool can help us get a better grip on reality.

The Expectation Gap

Almost every disappointment in life can be traced back to an unmet expectation. Think about the last time you felt disappointed. What played into your experience? Was your flight delayed? Were you craving seafood for dinner but served pasta instead? Were you hoping for a quiet date night after the kids' bedtime but interrupted by a sleepless toddler? Whatever the experience, an expectation gap leaves us upset. Without the skills to process the disappointment, many people live frustrated by a pattern of routine, unmet expectations.

The Nuts and Bolts of Expectations

Before we can get a grip on meeting or adjusting the expectations we have of ourselves and others, it is important to establish what those expectations are. The following three steps will help you outline and manage your own expectations.

1. **Identification:** Practice self-awareness about the expectations you hold.

2. **Communication:** Clearly articulate your expectations for others.
3. **Reasoning:** Logically explain the rationale for your expectations.

Identification

The first step for outlining expectations is *identification*: identifying what your expectations are and why you have them.

Lauren: In my daily routine, every morning begins in a similar way. I shower, style my hair, start boiling water for coffee in the kitchen, and then tighten the sheets on our four-poster bed. I arrange the pillows symmetrically along the headboard and fold and fluff our goose-down duvet. Walking down the hall past the kids' bedrooms, I never fail to notice sheets and pillows piled haphazardly on the floor. All my kids are capable of making their own beds, and when they do not, it sends me into orbit. Why does this bother me so much? My family deserves to know, and I am responsible for finding the answer.

My loathing of unmade beds stems from my own upbringing. Both my parents served in the US Air Force. In US military culture, bed making is not just a chore but a direct reflection of character. In his 2014 commencement speech at the University of Texas, Austin, Admiral William H. McRaven told the graduates, "If you want to make a difference in the world, start by making your bed." This speech has gone viral, with over ten million views on YouTube, and has been referred to by some of the world's best thought leaders. The admiral's view was shared by my parents and passed down to me. When my bed is made, I feel a sense of power and pride. When it is messy, I subconsciously believe that I have already compromised the day's success. Identifying the sources of my bed-making passion helped me understand why such a minor task has such a major impact on my attitude. Additionally, it has helped me acknowledge that even if consistent hospital corners are shown to lead to positive outcomes in other aspects of life, it does not follow that people who skip this task are less successful.

Identifying your own expectations requires self-awareness and reflection. Sometimes people carry the weight of consistent disappointment but feel stuck when trying to understand why. Many of our expectations are rooted in our childhood. The following questions can help identify your expectations.

1. What types of behaviors and patterns were prioritized in your upbringing?
2. What outcome did you experience if you did not behave according to these expectations?
3. What were you rewarded for?
4. When you dreamed about your future, what did you picture?
5. What hopes do you hold for your life now?
6. What messages from your educational experiences do you remember?
7. Which characteristics of your parents and family members do you want to replicate and pass on?
8. Which characteristics of your parents and family members do you want to change and not pass on?
9. What are three to five behaviors you observe in yourself or in others that make you angry?
10. What cultural beliefs or values guide your thinking?

Looking for patterns in your responses to these questions, both in your childhood and later in life, can help you discover why you hold specific expectations of yourself, your romantic partner, your family, and your colleagues. It helped me identify the roots of my frustration over bed making, revealing that my expectations are rooted in the values of military productivity and success. Before understanding the context of this expectation, I told myself a story that if my children failed to make their beds every morning, they would be more susceptible to failure in other areas of life. As it turns out, smooth sheets are not the sole predictor of positive life outcomes. I may always struggle to let go of the value I associate with perfectly placed pillows. For now, however, I choose not to let an unmade bed destroy my attitude.

Communication

Clear, direct, and specific communication is necessary if you want others to meet your internal expectations. We often falsely assume that intimacy and closeness give us access to one another's thoughts and desires. People often tell themselves, *If people really care about me, if they truly love me, then they will just know what I want.* We think, *I have a big life milestone coming up, and I really would like it to be celebrated well. I cannot wait to see what everyone has planned to surprise me.* But the milestone comes and goes with no pomp and circumstance. We think, *My efforts at the office have increased sales exponentially. I know I'm getting a bonus!* Months go by without any bump in our paycheck. Following such disappointments, we may pout with resentment and question whether anyone truly cares about us or notices our efforts.

Unfortunately, in this case, the responsibility is our own. Expecting people to read our minds is unrealistic and unfair. Clearly communicating our expectations, in specific, clear, and kind terms, makes it much easier for people to understand and satisfy them.

Joneen: Decades ago, when my children were preschoolers, I was invited to a friend's home for a brief visit. We had not seen each other in quite a while. I knew her home was beautiful and that she collected Lalique French crystal. I told her I could get a sitter for the children, but she insisted they come along. Sensing my concern about having three young children in the same space as her precious collectibles, she offered to child-proof the house by putting them away.

"Please do not worry about childproofing your home," I said. "I will ensure they know what is expected and respect your space." Before leaving home, I sat with the children on the floor and helped each of them put together a little activity bag with coloring books, crayons, puzzles, snacks, My Little Pony figures, Matchbox cars, and their own personal blanket. I told them that when we got to Mrs. Smith's home, I would find a spot for each of them to lay out their blanket. Once settled in their own space and on their blanket, they would find an item in the bag to keep them busy. I expected them to behave and be creative with their time. This visit would be limited to one hour. I took along a cooking timer and told the children we would leave soon after the timer sounded. I asked each of them to repeat what I had just told them to be sure they understood. Even my 2-year-old said, "Play on blanket, Mommy." On the way to Mrs. Smith's house, I repeated my expectations for their behavior. I also let them know there would be a consequence if they did not meet these expectations.

When we arrived at my friend's beautiful home, my children followed me like little ducklings. They responded politely to her fawning over them. When the pleasantries were over, I found a spot for each of the children, helped them lay out their blankets, and instructed them once again to get creative with the contents of their activity bags. I set the timer and went to visit with my friend. After twenty minutes of uninterrupted time together, she asked me in amazement, "How is it that your children are so well-behaved?" I told her they were just doing what was expected of them. When children know exactly what you are asking of them, there is a great chance they will meet the expectations.

Presenting the children with specific examples of the behavior I was looking for set them up for success. Had I simply turned around in the driver's seat and said, "Okay kids, we're here. Remember to be polite and don't touch anything," they would have tried to meet my expectations but likely would have failed. They needed to know exactly what "being polite" looked like. I gave them specifics: "When we walk through the front door, please go find Mrs. Smith, make sure you can see her eyes, and say, 'Thank you so much for letting us play at your house today.'"

Communicating my expectations with kindness modeled mutual respect and helped the children feel invested in meeting my goal. When we impose demands on others, or use a dictatorial tone — for example, by telling someone, "Get off the couch and help me fold the laundry" — their defenses go up, and they are likely to rebel or assert their own power to resist the demands. Being kind honors the person whose help you are asking for and demonstrates a healthy awareness of interdependence between parties to meet a goal. The same expectation reframed with kindness might sound like this: "Folding clothes is so much more fun with company. Can I please get your help for a few minutes with the laundry?" Some might call this flattery; we call it effective communication of expectations.

After expressing your expectations in a specific and kind

manner, confirm that your communication is clear. When I was driving with the children to visit Mrs. Smith, I provided a lot of details about how I expected them to behave. It was important for me to ascertain they understood what I was asking for, so I asked them to summarize what I had said in their own words.

Inviting others to restate what you have said confirms that your expectations are clear and reduces the risk of confusion that may leave the expectations unmet. Note, however, that this tactic works best in relationships where one party is clearly in charge. Asking a peer or romantic partner to summarize your words can come across as condescending or domineering. In cases where your relationship with the other party is more or less equal, consider qualifying your request for a summary with one of the following phrases that communicates mutual respect:

- You always seem to get me, so this is more for me than for you. Could you share what you heard me say to make sure we're on the same page?
- I know I can be long-winded. Would you be okay giving a CliffsNotes version of what I just said?
- Just to make sure we both understand how I am picturing it, can you tell me how you heard my request?

Reasoning

Offering a clear explanation of the reasons behind your expectations will help others understand, respect, and support your requests. In a work environment, supervisors should explain the rationale behind each staff member's essential job function by showing how the task supports the organization's mission. In romantic relationships, partners who respectfully articulate the reasoning behind their expectations help one another understand the value of the request. Among friends, explaining the reasons behind your expectations provides a pathway to greater intimacy and understanding. Reasoning enables others to see the heart behind your expectations and to feel that making an effort to meet them is worthwhile.

Lauren: My family often feels stressed by my expectations for a clean house, and they respond by withdrawing. This used to frustrate me, because when I get overwhelmed with house cleaning, I need and expect others to pitch in and help, not withdraw and hide from the vacuum cleaner. I've found that demanding that they help out is not a productive strategy. I have much greater success in getting my family involved when I provide the reasoning behind my expectations: "Hey guys. I've been feeling a lot of stress with all that we're juggling right now. Having a clean house provides a restful environment for me to feel at peace and calmer. I really need your support to help create this space. Can we please spend thirty minutes tackling the task as a team? It would really be a gift for me to have support with this chore."

Giving reasons is not magic: it does not eliminate my family's natural reluctance to do chores instead of pursuing their own occupations. It does, however, reveal a sound, logical purpose behind the expectation. Knowing the reasons behind a request helps motivate empathy and increase someone's willingness to meet or exceed your expectations. Consider the reasons behind your own expectations. If you find yourself asserting that other people should meet your requests "just because," your expectations may need adjusting. Prioritizing only the expectations that you can support with a solid *why* will likely lead to fewer expectation gaps.

Closing the Expectation Gap

Getting a good grip on what you expect from yourself and others is key for experiencing contentment and satisfaction in relationships. Without the ability to make adjustments when expectations do not line up with reality, people are left feeling disconnected and divided. Think about steel nuts and bolts, which come in hundreds of different shapes and sizes. No single wrench can be used on all of them, but an adjustable wrench allows widening or narrowing the jaw opening to fit a wide range of hardware. Now that you have sized and set your expectations, we will explore how to make adjustments in order to narrow common expectation gaps.

Lauren: TV ads for home improvement stores make me feel inspired, motivated, and creative, prompting me to set out to purchase a few gallons of paint for a room makeover. But when I get to the store and face more than fifty aisles packed with hardware materials, I feel overwhelmed. The commercials create the expectation that a brief trip to the store and a small purchase will transform me into Joanna Gaines of the famous *Fixer Upper* TV show. But the reality of the store setting reminds me that last time I tried to hang a floating shelf, I had to use an entire pint of joint compound to repair the holes I made in the wall when I failed to find the studs. I turn around and leave the store empty-handed.

In this incident, I confronted an expectation gap. My memory of a previous home improvement fail helped me escape the inevitable disappointment I would have felt after trying to upgrade my kitchen without expert help. Setting grand expectations comes from a noble place. We have been encouraged to reach for the stars, to go big or go home. We must, however, lower the bar when faced with reality, and let go of any shame associated with adjusting our expectations.

Many of us grew up hearing parents, coaches, teachers, or mentors say, "You can do anything you put your mind to." Unfortunately, this inspiring advice is false. I am five feet tall. I could put my mind to becoming a starting point guard in the NBA every minute of every day without ever having a chance of realizing this goal. Lowering our expectations to fit our real circumstances is not a sign of weakness: instead, it increases the opportunities we have to feel contented, satisfied, and loved. Throw shame out the window. Go ahead and tighten the screw on your wrench to narrow the expectation gap.

Applying the Wrench to the *Frozen* Plans

Let's return to my (Lauren's) daughter Lia's expectations for her birthday party. Her imaginative request set the stage for a monstrous gap between her expectations and my capacities as a mom to fulfill them. It was time to employ the Adjustable Wrench tool to avoid disappointment. Lia had done a stellar job in establishing expectations:

1. **Identification — Practice self-awareness about the expectations you hold.**
   My daughter knew that she wanted a *Frozen*-themed party. She loved the movie's storyline and wanted to replicate it on her birthday.

2. **Communication — Clearly articulate your expectations for others.**

    Lia was specific, kind, and clear about her vision. She outlined the details and gave context for them. She asked, "Can we please…?" and checked in with me at the end: "Sound good?"

3. **Reasoning — Logically explain the rationale for your expectations.**

    At age 4, Lia did not have the capacity to fully explain why she wanted this particular kind of party, but I could infer that her desires stemmed from imaginative childhood play.

Closing the expectation gap was simple. We held on to Lia's expectation by exploring what she loved about *Frozen*. We narrowed in on Elsa's dress and her long, blond Dutch braid. An Elsa dress hung in our basement from a previous Halloween, and I promised she could wear it for the big day. We recruited a few neighborhood high school girls with a knack for Dutch-braiding hair. To adjust Lia's impossible expectations of an ice castle, I gently reasoned with her, explaining that the weather in May was too warm, and that Anna and Elsa lived in Arendelle, not Denver. As we left the ice cream parlor, we had outlined a set of concrete, attainable expectations for an outstanding "Elsa Braid" party.

Lia invited four of her friends to sit on "ice princess" salon chairs (aka bar stools decorated with sparkly blue ribbon) and get their hair done in Elsa braids while wearing their favorite princess gowns. We will always remember that day as the birthday when expectations were met and exceeded, all due to the power of the Adjustable Wrench.

TAKEAWAY TOOL SUMMARY

Almost all disappointments can be traced back to unmet expectations. To minimize disappointment in your relationships, outline the nuts and bolts of the expectations you hold and share this information with others using our three-step process: identification, communication, and reasoning.

After establishing your expectations, measure them against reality. If there's a gap, be willing to engage the Adjustable Wrench without shame. Lowering expectations is not always unhealthy. In fact, doing so can often reduce disappointment and leave us feeling more satisfied and content in our relationships.

GIVING IT A FIGHTING CHANCE

 TOOL: Safety Glasses — Protect your relationships by learning to reframe conflict and see it through a positive lens.

We tend to believe that fighting is a sign of an unhealthy relationship. Couples who find themselves in conflict may begin to question whether they have committed to the right person. In a business setting, employees might contemplate leaving a career because of disagreements with a supervisor or colleagues. Believing that conflict is a fatal relationship flaw makes us vulnerable to losing relationships when there are signs of discord.

Yet navigating conflict is a natural and healthy part of life. To do so, we must learn to apply tools for handling it effectively. This chapter introduces the Relationship Essentials Safety Glasses as a tool for seeing conflict through a more positive and productive lens.

At The Center for Relationship Education, we have the pleasure of facilitating certification trainings that provide skills for building and maintaining healthy relationships. To set the stage for building skills to manage conflict, we ask, "What is the first thing that comes to your mind when you see or hear the word *conflict*?" Here is a list of answers from participants:

- fight
- run away
- tears
- anger
- hurt feelings
- hard
- distance
- scary
- yelling
- shut down
- avoidance
- silent treatment
- destructive
- fear
- stressful

This list demonstrates a broad consensus that conflict is a negative and destructive occurrence that must be avoided. This negative label is not limited to Western culture. A psychology research study conducted in Dalian, China, illustrates the universality of the human approach to conflict. The study's introduction notes the various terms used in the Chinese language to refer to conflict:

> In Mandarin, the following words are used to describe the concept of conflict: *wenti* (problem), *maodun* (contradiction), *chongtu* (clash), *zhengzhi* (dispute), *fenqi* (difference) and *butong* (disagreement). All these words have a strong hostile connotation and involve negative emotions in the Chinese interpretation. [Similarly,] in western literature, people view [conflict] as interference or blocking behavior, including negative emotions, such as stress, anxiety, depression and anger.

In our training sessions, once we have compiled the list of negative words associated with conflict, we discuss them in order to unpack some of the patterns that exist. These discussions reveal that the basis for the negativity stems from hurt. People avoid conflict because, often, conflict hurts our feelings. It hurts our pride. It hurts our egos.

However, conflict does not necessarily hurt our relationships. When handled appropriately, conflict has tremendous power to strengthen them. Before we explore this surprising truth, we invite you to answer a personal question: Why do you fight?

What was your answer?

We believe there is one universal answer: I fight because *I care.*

Notice that we intentionally pose the question as "Why do you fight?" rather than "What do you fight about?" This is important because, regardless of the surface-level details, people are willing to endure the negative and risky business of conflict only when (and if) it is over something they care about.

- If you are fighting about someone being late, *you care* about respecting other people's time.
- If you are fighting because someone spent too much money, *you care* about honoring a budget.
- If you are fighting about a political issue, *you care* about public policy.
- If you are fighting about an embarrassing social media post, *you care* about your reputation.
- If you are fighting about a window broken by a stray baseball, *you care* about your home.

Reframing Conflict

The list of words describing people's gut response to conflict indicates that conflict is associated with fear, stress, hurt, anxiety, and pain. We invite you to try on the Relationship Essentials Safety Glasses and look at conflict through an entirely different lens.

What if we told you that conflict is a sign of intimacy? You read that correctly. This paradigm shift requires a deeper understanding of what intimacy means. *Intimacy* is most commonly used in a romantic context to refer to physical (and often sexual) connection. Department stores have "intimate apparel" sections dedicated to skimpy silk and lace garments. Dictionary.com defines *intimacy* as "a close, familiar, and usually affectionate or loving personal relationship with another person or group." Synonyms for intimacy include *closeness, familiarity*, and *warmth*.

Expanding the definition of intimacy beyond physical, romantic connection is one of the first steps in shifting our thinking. We can and should have healthy intimate relationships not only with a romantic partner, but also with family members, friends, and even colleagues. In this expanded definition, *intimacy* means nurturing one another in a variety of relationship contexts so that we feel known, seen, loved, and cared for.

Redefining intimacy is an important first step for reframing our approach, but what is its connection to conflict? Remember that we fight because *we care*. Therefore, the people with whom we most commonly experience conflict often have the deepest knowledge of what we care deeply about.

Another way to better understand intimacy is to break it into four distinct syllables: *in-to-me-see*. Intimacy is an invitation for someone to see into our hearts, our minds, and our souls more deeply than other people. If we fight to protect things we care about, then we should care about who we fight with.

Intimacy varies with different types of relationships. On a scale of 1 to 10, our intimacy with a partner is probably close to 10. With our children, it's a little lower, between 6 and 7. With our boss, it might be about a 4; and with a grocery store clerk, it's likely about 1. If we have the same level of intimacy with a customer service representative as we do with a romantic partner or children, it indicates an unhealthy lack of boundaries (see chapter 3).

Lauren: I distinctly remember one of the first times I experienced an intense conflict with my husband. We were newlyweds in the honeymoon stage: time stopped whenever our eyes met, and we felt physical pain in our hearts when we had to separate in the mornings to spend our working days apart. In this stage I began to question all the relationship advice people had offered in preparation for our wedding, such as "Marriage is hard work," "Compromise is imperative," and "Love is a choice; you won't always feel it." Puffed with pride, and smitten with butterflies, I began to believe our relationship skills were more advanced than those of the people who offered this advice. Suddenly, however, we had our first big fight. We began to battle — hurling insults, raising defenses. *How could this be happening?* I asked myself. *We love each other so much.*

After fruitless attempts at conversation, we each went to a different floor of our house. We agreed that when we were ready to reconcile, we would return to the main level of the house and work toward resolution. Each of us waited alone and stewed. Hours passed, and no footsteps sounded up or down the stairs. That night we slept on different levels of the house.

I rarely experienced conflict with friends, and now I felt deeply conflicted in the relationship that mattered most to me. I later learned that this experience was not a signal of incompatibility but rather a sign of intimacy. Conflict with my husband mattered more than with anyone else because I have a more intimate relationship with him. Granted, we failed to employ many of the tools Joneen and I are sharing in this book, which could have helped resolve our conflict, but after recognizing that conflict intensity mirrors relationship intimacy, I was able to better understand that my husband gets to see more of what I care about coming to the surface — sometimes in the form of an argument. It was beneficial to understand that our conflict was quite normal; we simply needed to apply more productive tools in response.

A More Productive Approach

Transforming a conflict from disruptive discord to intimate discourse requires commitment from both parties to do the following:

1. Reveal what is driving the fight in you.
2. Lead with your brain.
3. Make generous assumptions about the other person.

Reveal What Is Driving the Fight in You

The first step in transforming conflict is to help the other person understand what it is you care so much about that you are willing to fight about it. In other words, explain your motive without expecting someone else to read your mind. Imagine that you are feeling angry and resentful toward a coworker about an imbalance of effort on a recent team project. Rather than passive-aggressively avoiding the person or making disparaging comments during water-cooler conversations, consider approaching this person directly and saying, "I recognize I have been a little short with you lately. I wanted to communicate that meeting our second-quarter benchmarks is extremely important to me, because our team success affects our chance of receiving an end-of-year bonus. I would like the whole team to pull equal weight. Your efforts seem to communicate that you don't care."

When you can articulate your *why* and show that you care deeply about an issue, other people are more likely to feel empathy or compassion. Both qualities are important considerations for respecting another person's perspective.

Lead with Your Brain

Conflict acts like a microwave for our physiology. We love how clearly Kirsten Nunez describes the multiple effects of stress hormones in her article for Healthline:

> During a fight-flight-freeze response, many physiological changes occur.
>
> The reaction begins in your amygdala, the part of your brain responsible for perceived fear. The amygdala responds by sending signals to the hypothalamus, which stimulates the autonomic nervous system (ANS). The ANS consists of the sympathetic and parasympathetic nervous systems. The sympathetic nervous system drives the fight-or-flight response, while

the parasympathetic nervous system drives freezing. How you react depends on which system dominates the response at the time. In general, when your ANS is stimulated, your body releases adrenaline and cortisol, both stress hormones. These hormones are released very quickly, which can affect your:

1. **Heart rate.** Your heart beats faster to bring oxygen to your major muscles. During freezing, your heart rate might increase or decrease.
2. **Lungs.** Your breathing speeds up to deliver more oxygen to your blood. In the freeze response, you might hold your breath or restrict breathing.
3. **Eyes.** Your peripheral vision increases so you can notice your surroundings. Your pupils dilate and let in more light, which helps you see better.
4. **Ears.** Your ears "perk up" and your hearing becomes sharper.
5. **Blood.** Blood thickens, which increases clotting factors. This prepares your body for injury.
6. **Skin.** Your skin might produce more sweat or get cold. You may look pale or have goosebumps.
7. **Hands and feet.** As blood flow increases to your major muscles, your hands and feet might get cold.
8. **Pain perception.** Fight-or-flight temporarily reduces your perception of pain.

Your specific physiological reactions depend on how you usually respond to stress. You might also shift between fight-or-flight and freezing, but this is very difficult to control. Usually, your body will return to its natural state after 20 to 30 minutes.

Understanding the body's physiological responses during conflict is important because it is nearly impossible to make rational, constructive decisions when the amygdala is flooded with stress hormones. Some social scientists refer to this phenomenon as the "amygdala hijack." Therefore, to lead with your brain during high-stress conflict situations, the first step is to walk away for at least twenty minutes to let the flood of stress hormones abate. Simply walking away from conflict often leaves the other person feeling unimportant or abandoned, so be sure to do two things before bolting out of the room:

1. State your motive for leaving: "I need a few minutes to process what I'm feeling right now, so I'm going to step away for a brief break."
2. Set a time in the near future to reconnect that works for both parties. "It is important to me that we prioritize a time to talk about this issue when I'm more capable of a calm dialogue. Does 5 p.m. work for you to reconnect and discuss?"

Leading with your brain during conflict also involves productively managing your emotions and creating emotional safety for both parties. Emotional safety is the freedom for individuals to express themselves authentically and display vulnerability without fear of judgment or control. An important factor for establishing emotional safety is debunking the categorization of emotions as good or bad. Anger, for example, is often categorized as bad, creating the false understanding that it is wrong to feel angry.

It is not when we *feel* emotions that conflict goes off track, but, rather, when we *lead* with our emotions. Consider the analogy of a freight train. It stays on track when the engine leads, the cargo cars follow, and the caboose trails at the end. Changing this order of the components, for example by putting a freight car in the lead, would result in a wreck. The same is true in conflict, when we lead with our emotions or act before engaging our brain. Anger, fear, and insecurity are all valid and allowable emotions, but we should not allow them to lead our decisions and behavior. Learn to lead with your brain, then process the emotions that follow, and finally take action. This metaphor can help you cultivate and nurture better emotional safety and keep your relationships on track.

Make Generous Assumptions about the Other Person

Becoming a parent drastically changes the rhythm and routine of a family dynamic. Many of these changes are magical and fulfilling, but some are challenging and create an environment that engenders conflict. First of all, having a baby disrupts the parents' sleep, and being tired leaves many of us more vulnerable to a big fight.

Lauren: My husband and I experienced this shift when our first daughter, Lia, was born. I loved having a spring baby because the weather in Colorado allowed for comfortable outdoor adventures. We spent the summer gallivanting through neighborhood greenbelts, pushing Lia in an off-roading stroller complete with a cup holder for my morning latte. My company's generous parental leave policy allowed me to enjoy many baby snuggles. However, as the weeks progressed, things got real. My husband and I have always both had full-time careers and a plethora of hobbies. Every fall for the previous six years, my husband had helped coach a nearby high school soccer team. We both knew the soccer season would take a toll on family time. My husband volunteered to give up the role for the year: "Lauren, we both know the time commitment coaching requires, and I don't want to leave you without support as a new parent." Although I loved him for this selfless gesture, it felt awful to see him sacrificing something that brought him so much joy. I steered our conversation in a different direction.

"Thanks for considering me. I really appreciate the heart behind this plan, but I would hate for you to give up something you love, and I will gladly step into the gap. The season only lasts a few months. I've got this," I insisted.

"Are you sure?" he asked.

"Yes," I assured him. I felt I had the parenting skills to handle the mom role while he spent time on the sidelines.

As it turned out, I grossly underestimated my ability to manage the newborn stress alone. On day 2 of practice, I found myself pacing back and forth in our kitchen with an inconsolable infant over my shoulder and a very disgruntled attitude toward my husband. I was accustomed to Josh returning home at about 6:55 p.m. By 7:03, I was angry, and I began thinking, *Why did I let him coach this season? Does he even realize what I am doing to make it possible for him to coach? I bet he is stalling on purpose. Maybe he took the other coaches out to grab a bite to eat after practice. Doesn't he know how much I value punctuality? Is he doing this just to make me mad? Come home already!* Caught in this spiral of negative thoughts, I heard the garage door open. I gently set our daughter in her bassinet and walked to the door, trying to hide my disgruntled state. The door swung wide open, and in walked Josh with a big smile, a breathtaking bouquet of fragrant red roses, and a card. I opened the envelope and read the following words:

Dear Lauren,

Thank you for sacrificing so much of your time to allow me to do something I love. You are the best!

I love you, Josh

My anger rapidly transformed into guilt. The whole time I was thinking negative thoughts about him, he was affirming positive things about me. Throughout the following days, the roses sat on our dining table as a tangible reminder to me to make generous assumptions rather than unfair and inaccurate ones.

Can you relate? Here are some other scenarios involving negative assumptions:

- You slam your brakes behind a driver stopped dead in the middle of the road, criticizing them in your head and laying on your horn, only to see that they had stopped to let a deer safely cross the road.
- When a coworker misses a meeting, you label them as irresponsible and selfish, only to find that they had just learned of a friend's sudden passing and were not in the frame of mind to prioritize work.
- A friend is hesitant to throw his credit card into the pile to cover the dinner bill after a night out. After you've silently labeled him as cheap and entitled, he confides in you that he was recently laid off.

Why is it that we frequently create negative storylines about people's intentions rather than giving them the benefit of positive thinking? One of the reasons is the "negativity bias" that is hard-wired into our brains. Margaret Jaworski explains this effect in her article "The Negativity Bias: Why the Bad Stuff Sticks and How to Overcome It":

Not only do negative events and experiences imprint more quickly, but they also linger longer than positive ones. According to researcher Randy Larsen, PhD, "This stickiness is known as positive-negative asymmetry or the negativity bias. In other words, for a multitude of reasons including biology and chemistry, we're more likely to register an insult or negative event than we are to take in a compliment or recall details of a happy event." The negativity bias can even cause you to dwell on something negative even if something positive is equally or more present. For example, you might spend all day with a friend and have a wonderful time, but if they make one small comment that perturbs you, you may end up remembering the day just for that comment — categorizing the experience as negative when the entire day was actually positive.

The Relationship Essentials Safety Glasses can help us think of others in a more positive light. Instead of internally disparaging someone's character when you feel conflict stirring, make an effort to think about their good qualities. When I was feeling resentful toward Josh, I could have reframed my thoughts along these lines:

- I know he recognizes the extra burden his coaching places on me and is making an effort to get home promptly after practice.
- He offered to take a break from coaching this season. I was the one who insisted otherwise.
- He cares for me deeply. I am sure he has a good reason for being a little late.

Positive thinking may not be enough to save us from all conflict, but the practice of making generous assumptions can help us cultivate relationship safety.

TAKEAWAY TOOL SUMMARY

Putting on your Safety Glasses enables you to approach conflict in a more positive way. Conflict is a normal part of every relationship. The presence of conflict does not indicate unhealthy relationships. What matters is how we respond to conflict. Put on your Safety Glasses to reframe conflict, lead with your brain, establish emotional safety, and practice the discipline of generous assumptions. You may find that taking a different approach to conflict can mean it brings you closer together rather than tearing you apart.

6

NAILED IT!

TOOL: Hammer — Aim to do things purposefully, with discipline and a plan. Intentionality will help you achieve meaningful connection and avoid leaving relational success to chance.

People are hard-wired for connection. Matthew Liberman, the author of the book *Social*, explains that "our [human] need to connect is as fundamental as our need for food and water." If this is the case, why do we leave relationship success to chance? At a recent training session, we asked the group the following question: "How many times, from your earliest childhood memories through higher education, did you receive formal education about developing and maintaining healthy relationships?" Most participants worked in vocational counseling or helping fields, so we expected their answers to be in the double digits. Surprisingly, the overwhelming majority answered, "Zero." Shocked, we responded, "Guess it's a good thing that you are at a relationship education training!" We went on to discuss the paradox that in a society that values education and skills, people are expected to just figure out the most important element of human existence — relationships — on their own. Relationship success need not, and should not, be left to chance. There are steps you can take to set yourself up to win. The Relationship Essentials Hammer tool will help you apply intentionality to your social experiences, increasing your power to "hit the nail on the head" and sustain rewarding relationships.

Lauren: If you have ever lost something valuable, you are familiar with that knot in the pit of your stomach that tightens as the search continues. In my experience, none of those knots compares to the one I felt one Sunday morning after clutching the handle of my coffee cup and discovering that my wedding ring was gone. Seeing the bare skin of my ring finger, instead of a round-cut sparkling stone, I was struck by panic. I set my coffee on the counter and gave myself an internal pep talk. *It's going to be okay. Take a deep breath. You are one of the world's best treasure hunters. You have yet to lose a sock in the laundry this year with a family of five. You will find your ring!* None of it seemed to help. I felt nauseated and foolish. How could I lose my wedding ring?

Josh and I found the inspiration for the design of my ring while strolling through an outdoor market after a brunch date one spring Saturday. Families sat around outdoor tables, shoppers walked by, couples passed us hand in hand. Just when I felt the day could not get any better, Josh stopped outside a quaint little jewelry shop and asked, "Want to look around?" How could I resist? The inventory was minimal, but the pieces were magical. The shop owner was an artisan who handcrafted each ring from his own designs.

Josh returned to the shop without me a few weeks later. The jeweler designed a delicate tiara setting for the center stone, capturing my Italian heritage and Josh's special nickname for me, Principessa ("princess" in Italian). The ring was a perfect complement to my great-grandmother's wedding band from 1921. When my mother gave me this heirloom and I saw the rings, old and new, together on my finger, I considered what they symbolized for my own marriage.

When I realized the ring was missing, I searched in silence for a few minutes, turning cushions and swabbing drains. I dreaded having to tell Josh that it was gone. But it didn't take him long to sense that something was off. "Are you okay?" he inquired. "You seem distracted." I had to tell him. I remember my voice shaking and tears welling into my eyes.

"I'm so sorry," I said. "I can't find my ring."

"Your wedding ring?"

"Yes. I've looked everywhere. I am devastated. I don't know what to do." My tears began to flow. Josh hugged me and said, "Everything is going to be okay. We'll figure something out." I wanted to believe him, but with zero recollection of when or where the ring could have fallen off and hours of fruitless searching, I resigned myself to having to replace it. With my family coming for lunch, I refreshed my tear-smudged mascara and concentrated on preparing the food and planning for a happy gathering.

Having company was a good distraction. I loaded the cooler with ice and checked to see if any of the food platters needed replenishing. Suddenly, I heard a high-pitched clinking sound. My brother was holding my ring above his spinach salad and asking, "Is this a party favor?" I leapt from the kitchen to hug and thank him. "Where did you find that?" I asked.

"It fell from the salad tongs when I was filling my plate." My ring must have fallen off while I was preparing the spinach salad.

The energy and intention that I poured into my search was a direct result of the value I placed on the ring. When we value things, we take care of them. Unfortunately, many of us have lost sight of the value that people have in our lives, and discounting their importance makes us vulnerable to losing the most valuable commodity of human existence — relationships. To honor and value relationships, we must make an intentional effort to cultivate connection.

Intentional Energy

When you swing a hammer upward, preparing to pound in a nail, the energy of your swing is transformed into potential energy stored in the hammer. When you strike the nail, that stored potential energy is converted into kinetic energy that drives the nail into the wood.

Relationships, too, require us to expend energy, in the form of intentionality — a commitment to moving your relationships in the right direction. Using the Relationship Essentials Hammer to apply this force toward your words and actions will help you effectively "nail it" in your relationships.

Be Intentional with Your Words

One of the greatest lies we ever hear originates on the playground: *Sticks and stones may break my bones, but words will never hurt me.* It's not true. Words have tremendous power to build us up or to tear us down. Picture a piece of wood in the shape of a heart. Think about the things people have said, either directly to you or about you, that were hurtful. Consider each as a nail hammered into the wooden heart, wounding it.

Sometimes, when people are made aware of the way their words have wounded others, they react with clumsy attempts to defuse the situation and retract their words. Are any of the following phrases familiar to you?

- "I'm sorry."
- "I didn't mean it."
- "I was just kidding."

We can think of each of these phrases as a metaphorical attempt to remove one of the nails from the wooden heart. But what is left? A heart full of holes. Hurtful words, even when retracted, leave holes in our hearts.

Joneen: In my child-rearing years, I tried a multitude of parenting tactics. I often felt like I was building the plane while it was flying, but I remember discovering one strategy that really worked to deter my children from flinging hurtful words. I invited each child to share what was said that hurt them. After the child repeated the phrase, whatever it was, I asked the person who said it, "Is that edifying?" My question silenced them (most likely because they had no clue what *edifying* meant). The question challenged them to stop and think.

Lauren: As a child, I recall hearing this question. "It depends," I answered. "What does *edifying* mean?" Mom went on to explain: "To edify means to build someone up and encourage them. Words that are edifying make people smile inside and feel good about themselves. Did you think that what you said to your brother made him smile inside? Did your words encourage him and remind him that you love him and are thankful that he is family?"

"No," I sheepishly muttered. "Not really, I guess."

"Well, then, the answer to my question is no. Your words were not edifying."

This simple question and vocabulary lesson helped make us more intentional in our choices of the words we used with family, friends, and even strangers. Knowing that our words had the power to either tear down or build up, we committed to building up. Now, even three decades after our childhood spats, I can still hear my mom's voice after I say something less than kind to another person: "Lauren, is that edifying?"

Most of us could benefit from hearing this question more often. Before speaking, ask yourself the question, "Is what I am about to say edifying?" and aim to make your answer an unequivocal yes. Harness the power of intention and transfer energy through your Hammer tool to strike your relationships with words that edify rather than wound.

Intent versus Impact

Lauren: In high school I played on the golf team. Golf requires careful focus if you are to have any chance of hitting the ball. My coach introduced us to a trick to help us focus on the ball: "When you set your golf ball on the tee, place the words (the brand name) facing up. Then, when you swing, read the words written on your ball before you look up to track its path. This will help prevent you from looking up too soon and missing the sweet spot."

I loved the way my coach took a general principle like "Keep your eye on the ball" and developed a specific way to help us implement it. Most of the time, it worked. Sometimes, however, even with the right focus and intention, my club face would hit the ball just slightly off target, sending a painful vibration through my hand and up toward my elbow. Something similar can happen in relationships. You prepare to strike your Hammer with great focus and intention, yet the blow causes a jolt of pain you never intended. In a relationship, either or both people can be hurt. If you feel like you "nailed it," but you discover that the other person is hurting, engage the claw of your Hammer, gently remove the nail, and seek to heal the unintentional hurt.

Over the summer, we championed our neighbors who took on a massive DIY deck project. As they hammered in rows of nails, some of the nails got bent out of shape. The distortions didn't show, however, because the nails were buried in the wood. When someone does or says something that hits you the wrong way, and you feel a bit bent out of shape, it is important to respectfully communicate the negative impact you experience rather than hiding your resentment. Simple and honest acknowledgment of your frustration helps prevent cracks of bitterness and resentment. Consider approaching the person and sharing your experience.

If you're the person whose hammer blow caused the hurt, it is vital to acknowledge the impact rather than minimizing it. Phrases like "I didn't mean it that way," "Don't take it personally," "It was an accident," and "I'm sorry you feel that way" dismiss the hurt you caused, even if it was unintentional. Try responding with empathy rather than defensiveness: "Thank you so much for bringing your frustration to my attention. I never intended to hurt you, but your experience demonstrates I did. Please know I never meant any harm." For healthy relationships to flourish, it is important to value the relationship over our individual pride. Clarifying our intentions, while giving others space to express any sense of hurt, helps safeguard connection.

Practice Intentional Decision-Making

Decisions should be supported by intentional thought. In relationships, learning to discern the *why* behind your decisions can make the difference between hitting your target and completely missing the mark.

It is estimated that the average adult makes about thirty-five thousand remotely conscious decisions every day. This sheer volume of decision-making makes it impossible to practice intention in all our choices. Bringing intention to bear on your relationship decisions, however, can greatly strengthen connection.

Replay a recent decision you made in one of your relationships. If someone asks, "Why did you do that?" how would you answer? If your answer is something like "Just because," "Because I had to," or "I'm not sure," you are likely missing out on the benefits of intentional decision-making. Employ our DECIDE acronym to help you make more thoughtful decisions.

Discern your *why*
Entertain your options
Consider consequences
Involve an objective third party
Defend your values
Examine past experience

Discern Your *Why*

Not all decisions are created equal. Some are easy, offering multiple pathways toward contentment and success. When decisions carry little to no risk, they can be made without a lot of contemplation. As the scale and risk involved in a decision increase, having a solid *why* becomes more important. Deciding not to indulge in dessert requires discipline and willpower, but if your *why* is to enjoy better health, the choice feels meaningful. To establish a track record of healthy decision-making in all areas of life, learn to apply discernment as a first step.

Entertain Your Options

Remember the catchy slogan from Reese's peanut butter cup advertisements, "There is no wrong way to eat a Reese's"? Similarly, when it comes to decision-making, we often have many options that lead to positive outcomes for us without hurting others. Yet we often defend our decisions by asserting, "I had no choice." If you truly have no choice, then the circumstance is no longer a decision-making option.

Acknowledging that we often have multiple choices frees us from the paralyzing belief that there is only one true path. I (Lauren) remember the excruciating stress I felt at eighteen when trying to select the right college. I landed at Texas Christian University, and I loved my college experience. To this day, I look back on my decision with zero regret and an abundance of gratitude. I truly am "Horned Frog proud" and am forever appreciative of the gifts of friendship, knowledge, and memories my alma mater provided. Even so, upon reflection, I believe I could have selected from a myriad of additional college choices and still have been happy and fulfilled. Freeing yourself from the stress that comes from having a "one right path" mindset enables peace and adaptability, which are both defining characteristics of healthy relationships.

Consider Consequences

Making thoughtful choices involves considering their consequences. We pursue pleasure and reward much more naturally than risk and cost. Paying attention to the latter, however, can vastly decrease regret and remorse later on. Imagine you are feeling angry after experiencing conflict with a friend. To "vent" and "process" your emotion, you type a disparaging text message about them and prepare to send it to someone else in your social circle to seek validation for your anger. Before pressing Send, consider the consequences.

High-stress situations, when emotions are running hot and adrenaline is pumping, impair the capacities of the prefrontal cortex of the brain. These include executive function — rational processes like planning, decision-making, problem-solving, maintaining self-control, and acting with long-term goals in mind. A brief pause to envision the negative consequences of pressing Send could make the difference between resentment and resolution in a friendship that is important to you. Rarely are we advised to think negatively, but in this context, envisioning the potential negative impact of decisions can protect your relationships from hurt.

Involve an Objective Third Party

Joneen: In my early twenties, after finishing nursing school, I thought it would be a kick to join the US Air Force. I had just completed the flight hours required for a private pilot's license, and my instructor told me that I would need to go to ground school to learn how to navigate. What better place to learn how to navigate an airplane than in the Air Force? I had seen ads in *Glamour* magazine about becoming a flight nurse. I contacted the recruiting office, and the next thing I knew, I was meeting with several Air Force recruiting officers who were trying to get me to sign up.

When my family and friends heard about this plan, they tried to talk me out of it. They had all kinds of stories about what happens to people in the Air Force, even though they had zero firsthand military experience. My own mom tried to talk me out of it through a psychic reading — yet I was the crazy one? Their opposition made me dig my heels in. My emotions were now in the driver's seat. Nothing was going to stop me from pursing this path. Validation from an objective third party would help affirm my decision in the face of family opposition.

I decided to call a high school friend's father. He was a quiet man who spoke calmly to his children, listened to them, and allowed them to express their feelings. My idea did not surprise him one bit. He understood and honored my impulsive and adventuresome spirit. "Let's do this," he suggested. "Stop by in a few days after giving it some additional thought, and we can process your options together." I accepted his invitation. Sitting at his maple dining table, he drew a thick black line with a Sharpie marker down the center of a legal pad. On one side of the paper, he wrote the word "Go," and the other side he wrote "Stay." He helped me outline my thoughts, fears, hopes, and dreams. The process provided clarity and focus. My spirit was soothed, and the confusion and anxiety disappeared. By involving a neutral third party, I was able to make a well-thought-out, unemotional decision. I did join the Air Force, and it was one of the best decisions I ever made.

Defend Your Values

Joneen: Two of my children lean toward more liberal political thinking, and two more closely align with conservative policy.

Their convictions are different, and that is okay. I can encourage all of them to explore their own values, but I lack the power to impose my personal views on them. We all have different values in other areas of life as well. It is important to know what you are naturally drawn to, what nourishes your spirit, and what you genuinely enjoy. It's also important to know what you cannot stomach. Have you ever ordered something off a menu that simply repelled you? Whether you chose to send it back or choke it down, your dining experience probably left you upset. The same happens when we make decisions in conflict with our core values. Honor your values when making decisions for yourself, and respect the choices of others when their values do not align with yours.

Examine Past Experience

When faced with difficult decisions, past experience serves as a helpful resource. However, the past only helps us when we are willing to look back and adjust the decision-making process that produced negative outcomes. Have you ever watched a bird fly straight into a solid glass window? Our family remembers a time where we watched the same bird fly at full speed into the same window nine times in a row. With every thump, the kids shook their heads in wonder. "Seriously?" they giggled, "how many times do you have to hit your head to stop flying into the window?" Thankfully, our tweeting visitor found his way to safer flight paths, but it took a lot of hits to redirect his route.

Have you ever felt like this bird? You make a decision that hurts your relationships, but you keep flying in the same direction and knocking your head on the glass. Intentional decision-making requires that we recognize past patterns that hurt us or the people we love, take notice, and change course to avoid repeated bumps and bruises.

TAKEAWAY TOOL SUMMARY

Employ the Relationship Essentials Hammer tool to avoid leaving relationship success to chance. By focusing on your target, you have a much better shot at hitting the nail on the head. Consider your words before you speak, focusing on the power of encouragement and edification. Practice intentional decision-making using our DECIDE method. Use your Hammer regularly, high-fiving the people you love. For impact, shout, "Nailed it!" after a job well done.

FINDING EQUILIBRIUM

 TOOL: Spirit Level — Learn to find balance among differences, and value respect over being right.

Relationships can sometimes feel like a crooked picture on the wall. If two people have strong opposing views, they may engage in a power struggle to prove that their way is the right way. The goals shift from equilibrium and peace to winning and pride. When we face differences in relationships, we must learn to balance opposing forces to achieve equilibrium. Otherwise, life becomes a constant seesaw of power and control. Using the Relationship Essentials Spirit Level tool will help you create balance in your relational experiences, even between strong, opposing views.

Lauren: Growing up in Colorado's Rocky Mountains, I rarely saw the ocean, but we enjoyed escapes to the Florida beaches on visits with Mom's East Coast family. Jumping over waves as they ebbed and flowed, I developed a curiosity about marine life and the things that lived beyond the shoreline. As an adult, I trained to become a certified scuba diver. My classes took place in the swampy, algae-ridden lakes of Fort Worth, Texas. My opportunity for open-water diving in crystal Caribbean seas came a few years later, when I traveled with my husband, also a passionate diver, to the Dominican Republic.

I had pictured a diving trip supervised by an expert dive crew, with a flashy boat stocked with top-of-the-line gear. Instead, we met one dive instructor who signaled us through a thick language barrier toward his three-person float boat. Its engine appeared rusted from the salt water, and the air tanks had the matte finish of an aging elephant. I had recently promised in my wedding vows to follow my husband anywhere he might lead me, but I was not so sure I wanted to follow him into deep waters with this guide. I mustered my courage as Josh held my hand at the edge of the boat. He counted, "Three, two, one, let's roll!" and we cannonballed backward over the side. I felt a stab of panic and squeezed Josh's hand for comfort. He pointed at my eyes, and then at his, to remind me to stay focused and breathe. At first I struggled to adjust my buoyancy control device, first floating too high and then sinking too low. When I found my equilibrium, the sensation was epic — floating carefree and weightless under the sea. Three bottle-nosed dolphins playfully circled us sixty feet below the surface. We swam over a massive grouper, speckled with glowing white polka dots. Fluorescent coral waved in the current. Pods of eagle rays spread their underwater wings, gliding right below our fins. I was hooked.

This adventure led to other vacations in dream dive spots, including Bonaire, an island in the Leeward Antilles in the

Caribbean. Bonaire attracts avid scuba divers from all over the world because it boasts many dive sites accessible from the shore rather than from a boat: divers can simply walk into an underwater paradise. From the patio of our vacation rental, a ladder led down into the water right over a stunning coral reef. A few days in, however, our dream vacation turned into a nightmare.

Josh, our friends, and I checked over all our dive equipment carefully, as usual. We submerged over the reef and descended slowly to our chosen depth of sixty feet. I was taking in the beautiful scene when I suddenly noticed a thick cloud of tiny bubbles behind me. I turned to see my husband rising quickly to the surface. I knew something was wrong, because he would never normally do this: rapid ascent from a dive is dangerous because the sudden change in water pressure around you can cause nitrogen bubbles to form in the bloodstream, leading to tissue and nerve damage or even death. It looked like Josh's buoyancy control device was malfunctioning and forcing him upward. One of our companions swam over and leaned on Josh's shoulders, kicking his fins downward, in an attempt to slow his ascent. They tried to dump air from his buoyancy device, without success. I realized I was witnessing a worst-case scenario. Josh surfaced with our friend, while I and another companion ascended more slowly, with safety stops every fifteen feet. When we surfaced, I saw terror in my husband's eyes. With great relief, we soon learned that he was okay.

Afterward we found that a grain of sand had gotten stuck in the valve of Josh's buoyancy control device, causing it to fill with air and propel him to the surface. Had the malfunction happened at a greater depth, the consequences might have been tragic.

The buoyancy control device keeps divers safe by allowing them to adjust their point of equilibrium in relation to the environment. Extreme shifts can be dangerous. In the same way, when we lose our equilibrium in relationships, our relational health is at risk. If too much weight is placed on one side of an issue or on one individual perspective, we lose balance. In these instances, we may win a lot of debates but lose a lot of connections. Using the Spirit Level helps keep us level-headed and helps us approach others on level ground.

Finding Level Ground

The physics of buoyancy has for centuries been incorporated in a common household tool, the spirit level, which helps the user establish a perfectly vertical or horizontal line. It consists of a long, straight metal or wooden ruler with a glass tube mounted on it that contains a liquid (the spirit) and a small bubble of air. When the bubble sits in the exact center of the glass tube, it shows that the ruler is level. Spirit levels are helpful for hanging artwork and floating shelves, ensuring that they are placed perfectly horizontal and avoiding the sense of disruption that comes from seeing things crooked or aslant. Similarly, establishing balance in relationships allows us to interact with others on the level, even when we find ourselves on opposite sides of an issue.

Leveling Personality Differences

Many of the opposing views we experience in relationships arise from differences in personality. Knowing something about our own cluster of personality traits and those of others can make us more understanding of these differences. There are a myriad of ways for categorizing personalities. At The Center for Relationship Education, we favor the work of John Trent and Gary Smalley, who applied the foundational principles of personality science to create a relatable and approachable personality inventory. They identify four personality types that they characterize with names of animals: Lion, Otter, Golden Retriever, and Beaver. To determine your personality profile, complete the worksheet below by circling all the terms that apply to you in your most authentic, comfortable state.

PERSONALITY PROFILE WORKSHEET

L	
Likes authority	Bold
Takes charge	Purposeful
Determined	Decision maker
Confident	Adventurous
Firm	Strong-willed
Enterprising	Independent
Competitive	Controlling
Enjoys challenges	Persistent
Problem solver	Action oriented
Productive	Leader

O	
Enthusiastic	Likes variety
Takes risks	Spontaneous
Visionary	Enjoys change
Motivator	Creative
Energetic	Group-oriented
Very verbal	Optimistic
Promoter	Initiator
Friendly	Infectious laughter
Enjoys popularity	Inspirational
Fun-loving	Flexible

G	
Sensitive feelings	Dry humor
Loyal	Adaptable
Consistent	Sympathetic
Nondemanding	Thoughtful
Avoids confrontations	Nurturing
	Patient
Enjoys routine	Tolerant
Dislikes change	Good listener
Warm	Peacemaker
Gives in	Steadfast
Indecisive	

B	
Enjoys instructions	Perfectionist
Accurate	Discerning
Consistent	Detailed
Controlled	Analytical
Reserved	Inquisitive
Predictable	Precise
Practical	Persistent
Orderly	Scheduled
Factual	Sensitive
Conscientious	Intentional

PERSONALITY PROFILE TOTALS

Count the number of terms you circled in each category, and write the totals in the corresponding boxes below. The category with the highest number is your personality type.

Personality Types

Lion

If you circled the highest number of words in the *L* category, your personality aligns with the Lion temperament. Lions are born leaders and are put in charge, or take charge, in almost any challenging situation. They live by the motto "Let's do it now!" which drives them to expect and desire immediate results. If a Lion is sitting on the couch and is struck with an inspiring home remodeling idea, they are likely to hop up, grab the car keys, and drive straight to the hardware store to purchase supplies. Sometimes they take action without consulting others. This behavior has the potential to cause dissonance and frustration in relationships with others who are hard-wired to process, plan, and take things one step at a time.

Our friend Kellyann is married to a Lion personality type and described a day over the summer when she came home from swimming with her children to hear crashing sounds from downstairs. She found her husband, Tyler, demolishing the basement drywall. "So, he just took a mallet and started knocking down the walls? And you were okay with it?" we asked.

"I was," she responded. "Granted, I was a little taken aback at first, but I came to terms with it fairly quickly. That's Tyler. He envisions things and just goes for it. Besides, we'll have an updated basement sooner than I thought, so that's a plus!" Her response indicated her knowledge and understanding of Tyler's natural temperament and wiring. Rather than making the impromptu remodel a point of contention, she gave him permission and allowed him to operate in alignment with his personality. "He may move fast," she concluded, "but I know I can trust him to follow through. He won't start things that he can't finish. It's who he is."

Kellyann and Tyler have more than a decade of marriage under their belts and a healthy respect for one another's temperaments. Even though Kellyann would have approached the situation differently, she values and respects Tyler's personality traits equally with her own. Therefore she was able to give him permission to be himself and avoided what could have been a major conflict.

Lions' unwavering commitment to their vision leads others to believe they have things under control, but it can also create the feeling in others that they are controlling. Lions are doers who are driven by opportunities for change. Because they are not afraid of peer pressure or confrontation, they may sometimes appear argumentative or proud. Pride is often considered a negative character trait, but looking at it differently might help you better understand the Lions in your life. Lions are the only animal group labeled as a *pride*. This is not because they are pompous, arrogant, or selfish creatures, but rather because they position themselves to protect their own at any cost. People with Lion temperaments are fiercely determined to care for their own. When this drive is misunderstood, they may come across as intimidating, distant, angry, or all three.

If you have a Lion personality temperament, take extra care to create emotional safety for others and communicate your motives for action.

Otter

If you circled the highest number of words in the *O* category, you align with the Otter temperament. Otters are fun-loving and optimistic, with extensive social circles and a knack for motivating others. If you have visited an otter exhibit at a zoo, or been fortunate enough to see them in the wild, you know that when otters are approached, instead of hiding, they tap into their playful energy to entertain onlookers. River otters have been observed to build slides down to the water in their natural habitats. Sea otters love to stay close together, even when they sleep, and sometimes intertwine their feet with those of another sea otter. As these energetic and fun creatures flip and twist through the water, they look around as if searching to make eye contact with onlookers for applause and approval.

Humans with an Otter temperament operate with similar traits. They love to talk and tell stories. They have twenty-five best friends but rarely remember everyone's last name. If you have a friend or colleague who has known you for more than a year but still only calls you "Bro" or "Bud," they are likely the Otter type. Otters bring joy, spontaneity, humor, and zest to relationships, and they are great optimists. An Otter's motto is "Trust me, it will work out"; however, they rarely have a plan or know for sure that this is the case.

Otters have a talent for making the most trying situations feel better, lending hope and perspective to others needing encouragement. If you are an Otter, however, it is imperative to exercise this trait with tact and a good sense of timing. I (Lauren) remember experiencing tremendous grief after the doctor was unable to detect our baby's heartbeat during a routine ultrasound appointment. After the loss, I remember someone with strong Otter tendencies saying, "If you can, try and remember that you have two beautiful, healthy children. This will help you keep things in perspective." Although the intent was to offer encouragement and hope, this remark came across as dismissive and painful. This perpetual posture of optimism and looking on the bright side is what makes the Otter personality style so magnetic, yet without proper discernment, Otters risk unintentionally hurting others. When Otters learn how and when to share their positive outlook, they are the world's best encouragers. We like to say, "Every office party needs an Otter." Their effervescence sparks a can-do spirit and inspires optimism in others. They are the type of people who believe in you, even when you don't believe in yourself.

Golden Retriever

People who score highest in the G category align with the Golden Retriever temperament. If you have ever spent time around a golden retriever dog, you know that they are by-your-side pets. Whenever you return home from work or running an errand, they greet you with tail-wagging and bottom-swaying excitement.

Golden retrievers as pets are fiercely loyal. They make people feel safe and model an unwavering devotion. The same is true for people with a Golden Retriever temperament. People in this category have hearts full of compassion. They will sit with you and listen to your troubles with endless empathy. They feel a strong drive to please others and put others' needs ahead of their own. Lauren's mother-in-law, who has a Golden Retriever temperament, stocks more than ten varieties of sodas, sparkling waters, juices, and beer in her garage refrigerator — not because she drinks them herself, but because she wants to be stocked with everyone's favorite. From neighbors to grandchildren, coworkers to perfect strangers, if you pass through her home, you are sure to be greeted with your favorite drink, a comfy place to sit, a warm hand-knit afghan, and a listening ear. Goldens are kind and present, thoughtful and accommodating. Everyone deserves to have someone in their life with this personality style.

Though Golden Retrievers have many positive character traits, they also have a few that may prove challenging for those who do not understand how they are wired. One of these is indecisiveness. Because they long to please people and are known as the peacemakers, they question every decision around how it will affect them, others, and the world at large. When asked, "Where would you like to go to dinner tonight?" a Golden will answer with "Whatever sounds good to you." When packing for a vacation, a Golden will likely require more luggage space to accommodate clothing and accessories for all possible weather conditions and an extra shirt in case someone they meet spills pasta sauce on their own shirt during dinner. Their indecisive nature stems from wanting to ensure that everyone has what they need and no one's ideas are overlooked, but it can lead to procrastination and second-guessing themselves that may frustrate other people. Golden Retriever types are at their best when prepared for change and acknowledged for their care and concern for others.

Beaver

Beavers are amazing animals with the ability to build intricate and stable dams using their teeth and tails. This creature, weighing an average of only forty-five pounds, can level sixty- to eighty-foot aspen trees. According to a US National Park Service publication, "Beaver dams do not just create a place for beavers to live. The ponds that beaver dams create are important habitats for other wetland animals, including birds and fish. These ponds also help control soil erosion and reduce flooding. Beavers are a keystone species. This means that they are important to an ecosystem because they modify, or change, their environment in a way that helps other animals and plants, too."

For people with a Beaver temperament, process is everything. Beavers go by the book. After purchasing something that requires assembly, the first thing a Beaver does is open the instruction manual to the inventory page. If the manual indicates that the item comes with 138 one-inch screws, the Beaver will open the bag and count all the tiny screws. If a single screw is missing, they will readily repackage the item and return it for a refund.

Beavers are not people who wear their heart on their sleeve. Rather, they keep a close watch on their emotions. They admit only a few into their emotional space — and only after they have taken steps to ensure that a person with whom they are sharing their emotions is trustworthy and safe. Those with a Beaver temperament make thoughtful and intentional decisions. They like charts, maps, and organization, and they require a noncritical atmosphere to do their best work. Because they value excellence and process, they have high standards and appreciate rules and consistency.

Joneen: I remember driving to a conference with one of my

colleagues who had strong Beaver tendencies. We were running late and hunting for parking. Looking at the situation from my optimistic Otter perspective, I glimpsed a parking spot right up front. The only snag was that there was a small orange cone in it. After looking around for a no-parking sign and not seeing one, I hopped out of the car, placed the cone in my trunk, and parked the car. To my surprise, my colleague was extremely frustrated with my decision and later told me that she felt it was disrespectful. I felt surprised and confused by this assessment until we looked at it in terms of temperament differences. I realized that what I saw as a creative solution to a problem was, from her perspective, a violation of process. A Beaver's motto is "Let's do it right." If Beavers operate without awareness, they may put process ahead of people. Of course process is important for maximizing efficiencies and optimizing outcomes, but always making it the priority can leave relationships at risk.

Balancing Personality Differences

Learning about these four distinct personality types helps us recognize the differences that exist in relationships. Lions, who value immediate action, are likely to experience strong opposition from Golden Retrievers, who want to be prepared for change and explore a variety of options. Otters may find themselves at odds with Beavers, who may question a spontaneous proposal to go skydiving by calculating all the risks associated with this activity. If we label any of these traits as inherently right or wrong, we lose our equilibrium. Successful relationships involve recognizing and balancing opposing forces.

Consider this example. Two colleagues are preparing to

purchase supplies for an office networking event. If one person has a Lion temperament, their aim is to locate, price, and purchase the items as if on a hunt for prey, speed-walking through each store. Their Golden Retriever coworker, on the other hand, wants to check out every aisle to ensure they select the best option. They make a mental checklist of all their colleagues' likes and dislikes. Hoping to accommodate all preferences fairly, they choose and reject items repeatedly until the final selection of purchases is just right.

Which person is approaching the excursion the right way? Is either person wrong for their approach to shopping? The answers to these questions are neither, and no. When people are made to feel right or wrong because of their different perspectives, relationships lose balance. Applying the Relationship Essentials Spirit Level to personality differences and placing equal value on different personality traits creates a level playing field.

Respect over "Rightness"

Recognizing personality differences helps us evaluate different approaches and acknowledge that each has merit. When someone desires pizza for lunch and another craves sushi, neither is right or wrong. If one person likes watching basketball and another prefers football, neither is right or wrong. Where we go wrong is when we value our opinions over those of others and dismiss the fact that an opposing view has any value at all.

Approaching people from a posture of respect over rightness creates level ground and enables people to live in balance, even in the most polarizing scenarios. Conversely, elevating rightness over respect puts relationships on a downhill path.

Seek to work toward equilibrium by accepting that differences are neither good nor bad, neither right nor wrong. Whether the differences are cultural, social, financial, emotional, or political, seeking balance will lead to more harmonious relationships and show the value of diverse thoughts and experiences.

TAKEAWAY TOOL SUMMARY

Balancing opposing forces in a relationship can strengthen the bond and create a climate of mutual respect. This requires treating all the people we encounter with dignity. Establish equilibrium between opposing forces, and value respect over being right. Many relationship differences can be attributed to individual personality wiring as well as to differences in culture, politics, race, religion, traditions, and geography. The Spirit Level is a tool designed to help us achieve balance even when people have diametrically opposite views and inclinations.

8

TAKE OWNERSHIP

TOOL: Scissors — Cut it out with the
excuses, and own your mistakes!

Owning our decisions and mistakes is a vital part of healthy
relationships. This chapter introduces the Relationship Essentials Scissors tool to remind us to "cut it out" with the excuses.

Lauren: Every so often I witness something while people-
watching that leaves me speechless, and not always in a good
way. A few years ago, on a holiday weekend, we visited the
playground at a park. Although it was crowded, parents and
kids were mostly friendly to one another, extending basic social graces and waiting in line patiently to take their turn on
the play equipment. A pig-tailed little girl in overalls raised her
hands gleefully as she reached the bottom of the slide. Before
she had time to stand up and move out of the way, another

child, more than twice her age, came down the slide and kicked the toddler in the back of the head. I heard the toddler scream, "Ouchy, Mommy!" and run to her mother for comfort. The mother stroked her daughter's hair and wiped the tears from her cheeks. She then took her by the hand and calmly approached the older child. She knelt down and said, "Hey, bud, I know you didn't mean to, but when you went down the slide, you hurt my little girl. It would mean a lot if you would apologize and tell her you are sorry." The mother of the older child came up, grabbed her child's hand, and pulled her away from the conversation, saying, "You don't need to listen to this woman's crazy talk. Let's get out of here!"

I was shocked. The mother's reasonable request that the older child own an innocent mistake and take responsibility for hurting another person was rudely contradicted by another parent. I felt like marching up to her and saying, "Cut it out!" If adults cannot model taking ownership for a small mistake on the playground, how is the next generation ever going to learn how to own their mistakes when the stakes get higher?

Cut It Out with the BS (Blame Shifting)

It is a natural human tendency to look around for someone or something else to blame for the struggles we experience. Have you ever been overlooked for a promotion and blamed your boss for playing favorites, when there might be evidence that you lack the skills necessary for the role? Have you ever sent an email asking for your child to retake a test they bombed, when it's possible that the child failed to study? How about when we blame our angry outburst on someone else's actions, which provoked us to snap?

The motive for shifting blame is simple: self-protection.

We tell ourselves that admitting fault tarnishes our reputation or diminishes our capacities in the eyes of others. Pinning the fault on someone else justifies our position and actions.

This strategy, however, rarely protects anything except for ego. One of the most productive paths to respectful relationships is to become aware of your own contribution to relationship discord. When you behave poorly, recognize it and admit it. Doing so sets a courageous example of transparent humility. It also communicates your ability to accept any consequences that result from your actions. The result may not always feel comfortable, but it will be honorable.

Two Forms of Blame: Accusatory and Excusing

Blame is rarely premeditated. It takes shape in the moment when our imperfections are exposed. We have observed two common forms of blame, which are both important to recognize and redirect toward personal ownership.

The first form of blame is *accusatory blame*. This places the responsibility for a problem on another person's wrongdoing. This strategy helps accusers position themselves as innocent victims. In some cases, of course, accusations are warranted — for example, if you witness someone commit a violent crime. But in the context of personal relationships, accusatory blame is a tactic more often used to manipulate a situation than to mediate it. If we blame our angry outburst on someone else's provocation, we may experience feelings of regret or embarrassment. Accusatory blame feels like a way to save face. "Did you hear what he said about my family? What a jerk. I mean, that's my kid he's talking about. He had no right to say those things, and I had no choice but to defend myself!"

The truth is, regardless of how negative or hurtful another

person's actions may be, the only person to blame for your own unhealthy reaction is yourself. To practice using the Relationship Essentials Scissors, take a step back from a natural tendency to accuse and express discontentment and own up instead. "I was so mad about the way they were talking about my kids, but my outburst was childish and over the top. Honestly, I am a little embarrassed. Regardless of what they said, I should have responded better."

A second form of blame is *excusing* — creating a storyline that justifies your actions. Unlike accusatory blame, excusing does not involve vilifying others; however, it still aims to protect ego and escape having to face the consequences of poor behavior.

Lauren: I have an uncanny ability to procrastinate when it comes to making and keeping healthcare appointments. I am fully aware of the need to plan ahead for my providers to work me into their busy calendars, yet I consistently find myself pleading at the last-minute for a provider to squeeze me in. Our healthcare plan offers us a bonus if our family participates in annual wellness checks. One of the required screenings involves a blood draw. Even though I was raised in a household with two parents who were healthcare providers, I faint at the sight of blood and run as far away from needles as I can. This may explain why I put off the appointment for my most recent screening until 8:45 a.m. on December 31 — the very last day before the benefit expired.

That morning, I woke up and began my normal routine: feed the kids breakfast, make coffee, and read. As I turned the pages on the couch, I caught a glimpse of the clock. It was 8:51 a.m., and I was not even dressed. I hopped in the car and dialed the clinic's appointments line. The only appointment slot they had left was in the afternoon. I felt angry and disappointed, because taking it would mean canceling a lunch date with a friend. I had been told that the clinic did not offer walk-in blood draws. Still, to avoid the consequences of my actions, I began thinking up any excuses that might persuade the clinician to bend the rules. *Maybe she is a mom, too.* "I had to step in for an epic toddler meltdown and lost track of time." She did not bite.

"I'm so sorry, ma'am, we're booked solid, and unfortunately I can't get you in earlier." *Maybe if I blame traffic she will understand.* I pleaded again, "I was en route this morning and got stuck in traffic. If I come in just a little later than my previous appointment, can you get me in between other patients?"

"I want to be able to help," she responded, "but there's just not enough margin in the appointment calendar." *Seriously, lady, you don't have ten minutes to flex for me?*

This would have been an appropriate time for me to employ my Relationship Essentials Scissors and say to myself, *Cut it out, Lauren! This is your own fault!* I waited until the last minute. My lack of ownership and sense of entitlement just made things worse. I truly felt like this clinic owed me a favor for my mistake. When I had to miss out on my lunch date, excusing blame immediately kicked into action, enabling me to convince myself it was the clinic's fault for disrupting my day. Can you relate?

No Matter How You Slice It, Bad Behavior Has Consequences

When I missed my medical appointment, the consequences were minor. I lost my opportunity to connect with a friend and most of my free time for the day. It is much easier to own smaller mistakes, because the consequences are manageable. Taking ownership for being five minutes late to a business meeting, for example, requires much less courage than owning a mistake that cost the company thousands in lost revenue. For relationships to be healthy and authentic, we have to own all our mistakes, small and large. Admitting to bigger mistakes carries more risk and, therefore, requires a tougher grip on your Scissors. Owning your part in challenging relationship dynamics requires courage, confidence, humility, and a sense of security. People who possess these character traits are better able to own their mistakes than those who operate from a posture of insecurity.

The Insecurity Drain

Joneen: Being a relationship educator, I handle a fair number of phone calls and meetings with individuals who, lacking healthy relationship skills, have experienced a cycle of toxic, hurtful patterns and desperately seek a break from the chaos. These individuals often feel possessive jealousy. They are hypervigilant about who their partner is with, who they are talking to, what they are doing all day, and/or where they are going. When I ask the caller if their partner has expressed love for them, they tell me that the partner says all the right words, but they do not believe them. Instead of recounting what their partner has said, they give me their interpretation of what their partner meant. These callers seem to want to convince me that their partner does not love them. As I dig deeper, however, I often get the impression that they are woefully insecure and do not love themselves. People who do not love themselves, or consider themselves unworthy of love, are more susceptible to relational discord. Consistent self-deprecating behaviors have the propensity to exhaust those trying to press in and affirm another's value. Healthy, affirming connection enables confidence and provides an appropriate setting for both giving and receiving respect.

Living in Security

Lauren: Embarrassingly, I distinctly remember moments when I created relational stress and hurt because of my own insecurity. In middle school, our cafeteria had a strict rule that limited seating at each table to six. I remember feeling worried that someone else would take the last open seat near some friends. To combat my insecurity, I solicited a vote to displace one of my friends who was already seated and eating. Instead of accepting that I got to the table too late and embracing an opportunity to meet new people, I deeply hurt someone else to look out for my own interests.

This incident happened decades ago, yet I still remember how my own insecurity drained me of kindness and sparked selfishness. When people lead from an insecure posture, their goal in relationships is not connection but competition and self-protection. Everyone is susceptible to feeling insecure occasionally, but if insecurity is a root piece of your identity, your relationships may suffer. An insecure identity puts people into "prove it" mode, hoping their accomplishments will demonstrate their value. This mindset initiates an exhausting cycle of striving and performing. Relationships should be something we get to enjoy, not something we have to earn. Start from a place of security. If you have ever felt (or currently feel) that you have little or no value, it is likely a result of toxic and unkind words that others have spoken to you. Begin to combat this invalidating speech and internal negative thoughts with the mindset that you have enormous value — not as a result of anything you have done or anything you will ever do, but simply from being human. This process can require time and sometimes even some outside support, but it is worth it!

In social situations, conversations often center on performance. People begin to broadcast their work promotions, describe all the skills they have that others lack, or brag about financial successes. Although there is great joy in celebrating life's accomplishments, performance and achievement have no relation to someone's value as a person. If you notice cues that someone is trying to prove their worth, try and interject statements that affirm and validate them. You might say, "You know that when you are with me you have nothing to prove, right?" Or "You realize you matter, even without a decorated résumé." A parent might say to a child, "The moment you were born we loved you, and you did not have to do anything to earn it. This will never change." These words bolster insecure spirits.

As people come to recognize their own worth, you can see the peace that fills them. Feeling valued jump-starts vitality, gives us energy to connect with others, and frees us from exhausting performance. A sense of our own value requires a mindset that sincerely believes "I am enough" without constant comparison to other people.

YOU ARE ENOUGH

The following exercise can help you develop a more secure mindset. As you read through the list of questions below, think about which ones resonate with you personally.

Being only five feet tall (like my mom), I (Lauren) sometimes internalize the question "Are you tall enough?" I also know I often lose my cool raising three children and working full-time. This leads me to question, "Am I patient enough?" Comparison and performance lead us to believe the answer to most of these questions is no. But remember that we discussed that value comes from our humanity and not our performance. This means that you *are* enough. To reinforce this idea, you'll change three of the following examples from questions to statements.

1. Are you thoughtful enough?
2. Are you smart enough?
3. Are you ambitious enough?
4. Are you tall enough?
5. Are you fit enough?
6. Are you quiet enough?
7. Are you talented enough?
8. Are you attractive enough?
9. Are you outgoing enough?
10. Are you social enough?
11. Are you interesting enough?
12. Are you rich enough?
13. Are you spiritual enough?
14. Are you emotional enough?

15. Are you logical enough?

16. Are you stylish enough?

17. Are you popular enough?

18. Are you funny enough?

19. Are you graceful enough?

20. Are you determined enough?

21. Are you sensitive enough?

22. Are you loyal enough?

23. Are you creative enough?

24. Are you relational enough?

25. Are you enterprising enough?

26. Are you confident enough?

27. Are you strong enough?

28. Are you competitive enough?

29. Are you goal-driven enough?

30. Are you verbal enough?

31. Are you friendly enough?

32. Are you adaptable enough?

33. Are you persistent enough?

34. Are you patient enough?

35. Are you kind enough?

36. Are you adventurous enough?

37. Are you brave enough?

38. Are you energetic enough?

39. Are you optimistic enough?

40. Are you analytical enough?

Choose three of the questions above. Convert each question into a statement by writing your name and the personality trait from each question in the blanks below (e.g., "Lauren is tall enough").

1. _____ is _____ enough.
2. _____ is _____ enough.
3. _____ is _____ enough.

As life progresses, this list keeps growing. Take time to remember that *you are enough*! Feeling enough lays the foundation of confidence and contentment in your relationships. If you are feeling the effects of insecurity in your relationships, consider a new mindset that acknowledges your value.

Cut It Out, and Go Make It Right

Most of us are familiar with a phrase like "You need to smooth this over." Even if the terminology you have heard is different ("Make it right," "Build a bridge," "Find a compromise," "Say you're sorry"), all of us have experienced situations that we were responsible for resolving. Smoothing it over sounds simple, but it is rarely smooth. It requires honest scrutiny and admission of your role. Owning a mistake wounds our pride and exposes our faults; however, it also enables reconciliation and provides us with a path toward peace.

"I'm Sorry" Doesn't Cut It

For reconciliation to be authentic, we must learn to turn words into action. When something you did or said hurts someone else, etiquette suggests you offer an apology. This often takes the form of two simple words: "I'm sorry." Unfortunately, it misses the mark. There are four shortcomings to "I'm sorry":

1. *I'm sorry* fails to take ownership of wrongdoing.
   If I catch one of my children hiding candy in their sock drawer, when we have explicitly set a rule that

sweet treats belong in the upper kitchen cabinet, "I'm sorry" fails to acknowledge that they defied a family rule. To fully express remorse, they need to own their actions as wrong: "Dad and Mom, it was dishonest of me to break the rule and hide the candy in my sock drawer. I recognize that was the wrong choice."

2. *I'm sorry* does not acknowledge the hurt or negative impact caused to another person.

Consider a couple fighting about a partner's decision to exceed their agreed spending limit on a purchase. This action will make it impossible to pay the next month's mortgage unless one partner takes on an extra weekend shift at work, forcing the cancellation of social plans with friends. Hearing the overspender say "I'm sorry" falls flat for a person bearing the consequences of someone else's actions. Practice full ownership by expressing awareness of those consequences. "I recognize that extra hours will cost you time away from friends this weekend."

3. *I'm sorry* fails to communicate an intention to change.

Without adjusting negative behaviors, people risk falling into cyclical patterns of hurt and destruction. Imagine a friend who makes humiliating and deeply hurtful comments about you in front of a family member. If they brush off the behavior with nothing more than "I'm sorry," you may feel vulnerable and skeptical about whether this friend will repeat this pattern. Taking ownership sounds like this: "I really crossed a line with that comment. I promise not to disparage you like that again, especially in front of your family."

4. *I'm sorry* does not invite or acknowledge forgiveness.

   For reconciliation to have a chance, an apology must enable the other person to offer forgiveness. Imagine an experience at work where a colleague lied to you about a missed deadline. "I'm sorry" is only part of the path to reconciliation. A more complete apology might sound like this: "I know withholding the truth put both of our performance reviews in jeopardy. I'm really sorry, please forgive me."

To help craft a complete, sincere apology we suggest utilizing a template called the Forgiveness Formula. This formula is structured to address each shortcoming of "I'm sorry." Filling in the blanks with content specific to your hurtful behavior (whether intentional or unintentional) will ensure "I'm sorry" is supported by statements conducive to restoration and healing.

The Forgiveness Formula

I was wrong when I _____. I recognize that my actions hurt you, and for that I am truly sorry. I will work hard to try not to _____ again. Will you please forgive me?

At first, this formula may feel forced or artificial. However, it provides a structure for taking complete, sincere, mature, and respectful ownership of mistakes. As you become more familiar with the structure, you can apply the formula in a more conversational and organic style. Applying the forgiveness formula with sincerity has the power to transform relationships and reconcile deep wounds.

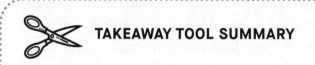

TAKEAWAY TOOL SUMMARY

It is important to acknowledge and own our role in relationship struggles. In every relationship, at least two people are involved. Therefore, both people play a role, even if it is a small one, in relationship breakdown. Ownership begins with awareness of your own wrongdoing. When you feel like hiding behind blame or an excuse, use your Scissors to cut it out and own up to your mistakes. Even though we possess a strong desire to appear unflawed, flaws are a universal part of being human. Work toward acknowledging your flaws rather than casting blame on others in an attempt to save face. Blame-shifting may protect your ego, but it fails to protect your relationships. Operating from a posture of security will help establish the courage you need to face consequences courageously. Fully apply the Forgiveness Formula, remembering that "I'm sorry" alone does not cut it.

9

GRATITUDE'S SUPERPOWER

+	**TOOL:** Battery — Charge your relationships with gratitude, which enhances both energy and positivity in relationships.

Gratitude is a superpower. Recently, I (Joneen) was rear-ended by an uninsured motorist after he ran a red light. My car spun 360 degrees and hit two trees. All the airbags deployed. Shattered glass blanketed the interior. My sunglasses flew off my face and were later found in the middle of the street by a police officer. My car was destroyed. Yet I walked away from the crash. As emergency responders approached the scene and asked me questions for the police report, I felt a wave of strength and an overwhelming gratitude for being protected from physical harm. "I am okay," I said in amazement, "and I am so thankful!"

In fact, I wasn't entirely okay. I learned after having X-rays taken that I had several broken ribs and two broken toes, along with cuts and bruises. When people saw the photos of my wrecked automobile, they gasped and asked me, "How did you walk away from that wreck?" But it was as if being thankful diminished the physical pain. That flood of gratitude sustained my energy and optimism for almost five days following the crash.

Lauren: I was attending a virtual meeting for work when my phone lit up with a text message from Mom. "Please do not be alarmed. I was in a car accident this morning. I spun around into a tree. The airbags deployed. I have a gash on my right eye and my left leg. I am very sore already. I just thank God I am okay." Hit a tree! Airbags deployed! How was I supposed to "not be alarmed?" I paused the meeting and checked in with my mom.

"Hey, honey," she answered.

"Are you really okay?" I inquired. "What you described sounds terrifying! How are you, no filters?"

"Just grateful, Lauren."

Gratitude is a quality woven deep into my mom's character. It did not surprise me that it trumped the fear, anxiety, stress, anger, and pain she might have been feeling. As I processed my own immense gratitude on learning she was safe, I felt refreshed, inspired, and empowered. That is the blessing of gratitude. The Relationship Essentials Battery tool represents the lasting power that gratitude brings to relationships.

A Global Perspective

Joneen: Traveling is a true gift that has exposed me to cultures and people I would never have had the opportunity to know. One of my most endearing adventures was on a visit to Kenya, when I was introduced to some of the residents of a Maasai village. Walking through rows of mud huts with thatched roofs, I observed a sense of contentment and joy different from anything I had experienced in the United States, and a gratitude for the simplest things, such as clean water and one hearty meal a day. Even in the face of scarcity, they graciously shared what they had with their guests.

The traveling I have done among Westerners has sometimes offered a stark contrast. I enjoy cruises that visit many different ports. There is so much to do and so much to see, and the gentle rocking of the ship helps me catch up on sleep. Yet some of the guests seem not to realize how fortunate they are to be able to travel in this style. At dinner one night on a cruise through the Caribbean, I listened to adults behaving like preschoolers who had not learned basic manners. "Gimme this, gimme that," they demanded. I felt bad for the food service staff, who kept smiling despite the disrespectful treatment. When I saw examples of more gracious behavior, like passengers phrasing their requests as "May I please have..." and thanking the staff, I thought, *This is a person I would like to know*. Gratitude energizes us.

Gratitude as a Mindset

Joneen: While raising my children, I was keenly aware of their acute concern for fairness. Each noticed what the others were given and was quick to call out any differences. Once, when dishing out M&M's as an after-dinner treat, I placed four ceramic ramekins in a line. The children waited patiently as I dropped the candies one at a time into each ramekin, giving every kid exactly fifteen. I can still hear the candy clinking against the ceramic dishes. "That should do it!" I said. "Enjoy!"

I watched the kids count to be sure the distribution was fair. *No complaints today*, I thought to myself. *This plan was genius.* Suddenly I heard one of them pipe up, "Mom?"

"Yes, honey. How can I help?"

"How come she has more green ones than I do?"

Are you serious? I thought.

"That's it," I said. "If you cannot be grateful for what you were given, without comparing between your brothers and sisters, no one gets any candy at all!" I gathered the candy dishes and dumped them into the trash can. The kids lost their dessert, and I lost my patience. What we gained, however, was awareness about how easy it is to feel entitled and how important it is to redirect that mindset toward gratitude.

Later I explained to them that every child of mine deserved to experience good things — not because of anything they did, but because they were loved. "I love you," I told them. "The love I have for you compels me to be generous toward you. I want you all to enjoy the things I give you and receive them with a thankful heart." I went on to explain that comparing what others have to what they have misses the point. Gratitude starts when you recognize that the things you want or need are right in front of you, and it grows when you understand how truly sweet that gift is. Losing their M&M's reminded the kids that life is sweeter with chocolate. They acquired new understanding of the importance of a grateful heart. "I never owed you candy," I said. "I provided it for you from a place of generosity and kindness. Next time, please just say thank you!"

The Origins of Entitlement

As older generations observe those that follow, they say things like, "Kids these days are so entitled. They expect everything to just be handed to them with no hard work, no sweat equity, and no commitment." Entitlement, however, is not a generational problem; it is a universal human problem. All of us, young and old, carry a sense of what we want and believe we deserve. Of course, some people do display extremes of entitled thinking (expecting six-figure salaries and paid vacation during a college internship, for example), but they are outliers. Entitlement is a mindset rather than a character flaw. At its core, it is a fight for liberty and justice. Diane Barth, a licensed counselor of social work and a contributor to *Psychology Today*, has a helpful perspective on entitled thinking:

> Sometimes a sense of entitlement can emerge from feelings of being mistreated or not getting what we need. It can be a way of saying, "I deserve to be taken care of, or treated with compassion and respect, just as much as anyone else does." Often individuals who have been mistreated or disrespected exhibit a sense of entitlement when they start to feel that they deserve better than they have been getting. This is part of a healthy shift towards self-respect. Yet they, too, eventually need to find a way to balance self-respect with respect for others.

Linking entitled thinking to a desire for respect and dignity is a useful reframing, one that can help us empathize with others' needs and feel a closer connection to them. Connection in turn energizes a force for good and a desire to help all human beings feel respected and valued. When we isolate and place people into unequal categories, we lose the power of relationship. Awareness of the humanity of others, and learning to see their inherent value, leads to gratitude.

The first step toward cultivating gratitude is acknowledging a desire and need for the people in your life. We depend on one another for survival. If humans possessed the capacity to live alone, we would be like octopuses, who die after laying their eggs and whose offspring are left to their own devices to survive. Interdependence and togetherness are special and precious qualities of human existence. Capacity for gratitude in relationships requires that we understand and embrace the importance of having others in our lives.

The Power of Together

Lauren: Fall is my favorite time of year, not only because it includes my birthday month (remember how much we both love birthdays!) but also because of the magnificent golden hues of Colorado's aspen forests as the leaves turn and fall, contrasting with the chalky-white bark of their trunks and the vivid blue of the sky. The quaking of the long-stemmed leaves in the wind gives the species its formal name, the quaking aspen. One equally striking but less obvious characteristic of aspen forests is that all the trees in a forest are interconnected, sharing a single root system. A cluster of aspen trees is called a clone, and one clone in Utah has been referred to by scientists as one of the world's largest single living organisms. Called Pando, the clone comprises approximately forty-seven thousand genetically identical quaking aspens, all stemming from one root system.

One or two aspen trees in a backyard landscaping project, by contrast, are unremarkable. Sure, their colors still change, but you hardly notice. Aspen trees evolved to blanket the mountains by the thousands, where they captivate us with their beauty. In the same way, humanity presents its best and strongest nature when people live in connection, linked by a strong foundation. When we isolate ourselves, relationships suffer.

Consider the people in your relationship cluster. Do you feel linked at your roots? Do you allow others to know and help meet your needs? Or are you more of a solitary sprout, refusing even to let people know your needs, let alone meet them? As we learn to plug into relationships and community for support, we enhance both our power for good and the gratitude we express toward others. Everyone is born into this world completely dependent on others to sustain life and support their growth. As we grow and learn to stand on our own two feet, we exert independence and want to do more on our own. Although increasing self-reliance is necessary as we mature, it is important never to lose sight of the human needs that can only be fulfilled through relationship.

The Power Drain of Independence

Joneen: Early in my marriage, I was impressed whenever my husband made me a meal. He came up with a plan, shopped for fresh ingredients, and set the table with care. It felt like royal treatment. What a delight it was to have married someone who loved to prepare and serve wonderful meals. I regularly thanked him for all his efforts.

Additionally, we loved cooking and entertaining dinner guests. As time went on, however, I went from appreciating my husband's passion to feeling entitled to and sometimes even annoyed by it. The extravagant dinner spread and presentation took too much energy to acknowledge when I felt hungry and tired and just wanted a quick, easy meal. A gracious and much-appreciated gesture turned into a frustration.

What happened? As relationships progress, people tend to slide into complacency, often forgetting to feel and express gratitude for other people's contributions to their routines. The new hire at work, who at first received praise and affirmation for a job well done, now, three years in, is no longer noticed but just expected to do the work perfectly. The couple who previously delighted in sharing household chores suddenly start keeping mental scorecards of tasks left undone or unappreciated. The friend who routinely used to make time to check in is now, after a life transition, too busy to schedule a lunch date. Over time, we often lose sight of our need for one another and the power of expressing gratitude when those needs are met. Giving becomes a burden rather than a joy.

Healthy interdependence enables both having needs and being needed. And gratitude is best felt and expressed when we recognize that our needs are being met. Expressing need, and being receptive to receiving help, cultivates gratitude. Nothing melts a parent's heart more than when a child requests, "Help me, please." Working together to meet an expressed need is the foundation of relationships. If we try to get by with meeting our own needs and disregarding the needs of others, the power of gratitude drains from our battery. We can run for a while, but eventually the battery runs out.

At first, self-reliance feels empowering, affirming our capacity to thrive alone. If taken too far, however, it cuts us off from our shared root system. A voice starts to whisper, "Life would be so much simpler if I did not have to deal with all these people. I do not need anyone." Sure, we can still live productive and healthy lives, but like the lone quaking aspen in the backyard, we lose the brilliance that comes from being part of a community.

Lauren: I think of my youngest child, Nina, who is fiercely independent. She wants to do everything without assistance and takes great pride in saying, "All by myself!" Ironically, though, her accomplishments fall flat when no one is around to witness and share in her success. It has been fun to watch her observe and emulate more productive behaviors that she has picked up from her older siblings. Her brother, Jace, routinely asks, "Mom, how can I help? — a question that prompts the very best version of me as a parent. This desire to serve solicits similar benefits in all relationships. As we learn to surrender our fight for independence, our root system grows and produces more abundant connections in families, businesses, and communities. If complete independence were the norm, we would all stand alone like solitary, lackluster aspen trees. Acknowledging healthy needs in our lives, and expressing appreciation toward those who help us meet them, is key for keeping our batteries charged with gratitude.

Gratitude Powers Resilience

Throughout life, every one of us will encounter negative and challenging circumstances. There is no perfect strategy for avoiding pain, but there is a strategy we can employ to face it. Studies demonstrate that feeling gratitude in the face of adversity and pain can make the difference in overcoming it. Fill in the battery diagram on the next page with experiences, both positive and negative, that have shaped your life. List the positive milestones toward the top and the negative ones toward the bottom.

MY LIFE EXPERIENCES

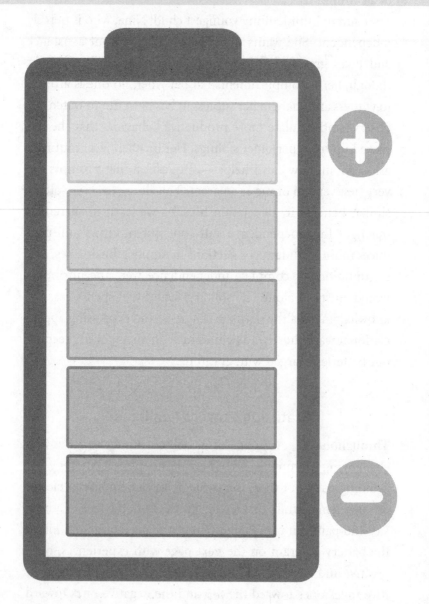

Recalling life's challenges can be painful (and we want to express our gratitude to you for taking on the task). When life throws curve balls, people generally adopt one of two outlooks: *victim* or *victor*. If you have been the victim of any unhealthy life event, we want to stop, acknowledge and empathize with your pain, and affirm that no one ever deserves to be victimized. We also want to encourage you, however, not to stay trapped and give that posture more power than it deserves.

A circumstance that causes someone to be victimized can sometimes produce a double foul by trapping them into staying stuck. This is a case of the victim *experience* becoming a victim *identity*. "I feel helpless, or I feel stuck" changes to "I am helpless. I am stuck!" Adopting the victim identity can lead a person to develop a downtrodden, woeful outlook that is draining and challenging for others to be around. The world is forever gray, and nothing anyone says has the power to help. Think of Eeyore, the donkey from *Winnie-the-Pooh*, who carries a cloud over his head everywhere he goes. The victim mindset can drain the energy from any relationship.

Just a small shift can change *victim* to *victor*. *Victor* defines someone who overcomes an enemy or opponent. When faced with a seemingly impossible challenge, victors devote their mind and attitude toward overcoming it. Consider the Super Bowl LII champions, the Philadelphia Eagles. Going into the game as significant underdogs, they achieved victory over the five-time champion New England Patriots. In postgame interviews, Eagles players continually expressed gratitude for, and affirmation of, the teammates, coaches, and communities who stood by them.

The road to the championship was paved with challenges. As a franchise, the Eagles have lost more games than they have won, and they waited fifty-seven years for a chance to hold the

Vince Lombardi Trophy. As they accepted the trophy, their raw emotion and abundant gratitude were evident.

We laud and celebrate victories but rarely stop to acknowledge the hardship that paved the way to triumph. Justin Bariso captured the moment in an article he wrote for Inc.:

> As [Eagles quarterback Nick] Foles stood for his interview as Super Bowl MVP, he could have told us that he knew all along he would make it here. He could have told us how he deserved to be on this stage, and that he never lost belief in himself, or doubted his abilities. He could have told us that, but he did not. Because as he knew more than anyone, those things would not be true. Instead, Foles reminded us that as recently as a couple of years ago, he almost gave up on football. As he shared his struggle, he was calm and collected.

According to Bariso, Foles's perseverance teaches a valuable lesson about the resilience that can emerge from even the greatest challenges. No one ever predicted he would be the newest Super Bowl MVP, "perhaps not even Foles himself."

Even in the most challenging circumstances, gratitude can make the difference between succeeding and being forever stuck.

> Social scientists have been studying gratitude intensively for almost two decades, and have found that it produces a remarkable array of physical, psychological, and social changes. Robert Emmons of the University of California at Davis and Michael McCullough of the University of Miami have been among the most prolific contributors to this effort. In one of their collaborations, they asked a first group of people to keep diaries in which they noted things that had made them

feel grateful, a second group to note things that had made them feel irritated, and a third group to simply record events. After 10 weeks, the researchers reported dramatic changes in those who had noted their feelings of gratitude. The newly grateful had less frequent and less severe aches and pains and improved sleep quality. They reported greater happiness and alertness. They described themselves as more outgoing and compassionate, and less likely to feel lonely and isolated. No similar changes were observed in the second or third groups. Other psychologists have documented additional benefits of gratitude, such as reduced anxiety and diminished aggressive impulses.

It is more common, and easier, to feel annoyed or irritated by the people around us than it is to feel gratitude toward them. It feels more satisfying to complain about an overbearing boss in the break room than it does to identify and affirm their talents and contributions. With loved ones, we may get stuck in thinking critically about the things they forget to do instead of acknowledging what they contribute to our lives, often behind the scenes. Left unchecked, these complaints nurture a victim mindset, leaving us feeling that everyone is against us. Conscious effort is required to transform this victim mindset into a victor mindset.

Is a lack of gratitude keeping you stuck as a victim? You can supercharge your path toward a victor perspective by practicing gratitude routinely. Best practices include keeping a gratitude journal, mailing handwritten thank-you notes, and intentionally expressing appreciation for others. An infusion of gratitude can be just the power you need to recharge your battery.

⊞ TAKEAWAY TOOL SUMMARY

A mindset of gratitude can often make the difference between feeling powerful and powerless in relationships. Gratitude projects a refreshing and vibrant energy that attracts other people. Refresh and recharge often by expressing your needs, acknowledging your interdependence with others, and allowing others to help meet those needs as you help meet theirs. Independence is a signal of strength, but taken to an extreme, it can drain your battery and leave you isolated and disconnected. Being grateful is a strategy for developing resilience, as we naturally feel grateful when we have overcome adversity. Recharge your connections with your Relationship Essentials Battery tool.

10

THE VIEW
FROM THE TOP

 TOOL: Extension Ladder — Distance
yourself from everyday stress to gain a
higher perspective and keep relationship
success in sight.

Continual stresses and challenges can exhaust the energy
required to maintain healthy relationships. Without a strategy, we tend to feel more distant and alone over time instead
of connected and attached. Looking at things from a higher
perspective breathes new life into our relationships. This final
chapter introduces the Relationship Essentials Extension Ladder as a way to gain perspective and enable your relationships
to reach new heights.

Joneen: I will never forget the day I learned that a life-
long friend had been diagnosed with a fatal illness. Days
after celebrating my sixtieth birthday, I found myself feeling
grief-stricken and vulnerable. Craving new hope and a higher

perspective, I signed up for a skydiving lesson. I felt I needed to get above it all.

The sales representative at the Mile High Sky-Diving Center processed my payment and reminded me that there were no refunds. I was committed. To have some company in the experience, I invited a friend (who also needed a little wind in her sails) to come along. On the drive north, the thrill of adrenaline warred with trepidation, producing a knot of emotions in my gut. "Are we doing this? For real?" I asked.

"No turning back now!" responded my friend, and we were off. To avoid tightening that knot in the pit of our stomachs, we grabbed a bite to eat. The food met our fear, and we tossed our cookies! "All clear now," we joked and pulled into the gravel parking lot. An oversized tram pulled up in front of our car. "Hop on in," the driver instructed. Once we reached the terminal, several young instructors wearing smiles and flight suits came out to greet us. *Maybe I am too old for this*, I thought to myself. Then, *Nope — this is the kind of thing that will keep me young; I am all in!* We signed our lives away in waivers. Approaching the plane, we asked one another one last time, "Are we crazy? Do we really want to do this?" With an enthusiastic yes to both questions, we were off.

Once we were in the air, seated on a metal bench, the noise of the doorless plane prevented conversation. My guide gave a thumbs-up, signaling it was go time. Letting go of the door frame, we launched into the open air, 8,500 feet above the ground. Crisp mountain air pushed against my face, tightening my wrinkles. *What is a 60-year-old grandma doing here?* The free fall was surreal and exhilarating. We twisted and turned like acrobats, reveling in the eagle's-eye view. My guide counted "Three, two, one," and then pulled the parachute handle. I felt a jolt, and then we were gliding. It was heavenly. As I looked around, wonder replaced exhaustion in my spirit. Ten minutes later, we prepared for the landing. My guide adjusted his position to absorb the impact. I lifted my heels as we sailed gracefully to the ground, feeling a rush of pure joy.

That day, we overcame life's defeats and gained higher ground and much-needed perspective. We picked up our certificates and the video proving that we had done this crazy thing, hung around until our adrenaline levels had dropped a bit, and headed for the car. Back on the tram we high-fived others, sharing the thrill of adventure. Looking down at the world from 8,500 feet, the weight of my circumstances felt manageable, even if only for a short time. What seemed so big from land was tiny from above.

What kind of weight are you carrying in your relationships? Burdens like critical illness or the loss of a job can prevent us from seeing beyond our immediate circumstances and steal our hope. Lighter burdens, such as the annoying habits of others or piles of unfolded laundry, can also hamper relational bliss. Viewing things from a higher plane enables us to see beyond the struggle. Boulders can look like pebbles. Fresh air can enter back into our lungs. A fresh perspective can lift our hearts.

Too Close to the Situation

Lauren: My kids like to mess with me in the morning. Sometimes they tiptoe to the edge of our bed, lean in just centimeters away from my face, and stare. The sensation of their warm morning breath disturbs my sleep, and — *wham!* — I wake up, terrified, to see two beady eyes staring me down. Every time, I scream, and they burst into giggles. "We got you again, Mom!"

"Yes, you did," I grumble. "Now who is going to make it up to me by making breakfast?"

You would think this repeated stunt would teach me not be afraid or react, but it always elicits the exact same response. When the kids stare at me from so close, all I see is a dark mass hovering over my face, and I react in fear. The same thing can happen in life. Seeing a menacing shape looming right in front of us, we react by taking fright and pushing people away, thinking, *Get out of my face.* In times of intense stress or grief, we can miss opportunities to deepen relationships. According to the American Institute of Stress, "More than a quarter of people in a recent survey felt alienated from a friend or family member because of stress, and over half had fought with people close to them." Without some space and perspective, we withdraw from the very people we love and who often can help us. Without distancing ourselves from certain situations, we cannot maintain focus on the essentials or the people in our lives.

When something is too close for us to focus on it, it strains and blurs our vision. An understanding of the physical strain on our eyes helps depict the emotional strain on relationships. A professor of anatomy explains that "the muscles that control the shape of the lens are called ciliary muscles. When you are looking at an object far from you, like the building out your window, the ciliary muscles around your eye are relaxed, the lens is stretched out, and the fibers around the eye are tight. This maximizes your ability to see objects at a distance clearly." Conversely, when we are too close to something, the ciliary muscles become tense and strained in their attempt to focus. The solution is to take a step back.

The same is often true in relationships. If we can distance ourselves from the short-term stress in our circumstances, we can relax and get a clearer view of what's needed for relational health. The Extension Ladder tool provides a practical strategy for gaining higher ground.

Preparing for the Ascent

Being short, we both regularly need assistance to reach things up high. A small step stool usually does the trick for accessing kitchen shelves, but it doesn't extend our reach or perspective very far. Follow these steps for ditching the step stool and reaching greater heights with the Extension Ladder.

To engage your ladder:

1. Establish a secure foundation.
2. Climb one step at a time.
3. Keep looking up.

Establish a Secure Foundation

A firm foundation is vital for stability and safety. A ladder must be set on a level, stable surface. Likewise, a relationship must be set on a foundation of trust, respect, and support. When any one of the three is missing, relationships are vulnerable to collapse. All too often, we look at these character qualities and overcomplicate them. We urge you to simplify your approach with a quick yes-or-no test.

Consider a person with whom you have a relationship.

- Do you trust this person?
- Do you respect this person?
- Do you support this person?

Many of us vacillate, answering these questions with a maybe. I remember speaking with a young couple preparing to get married. When I asked, "Do you trust each other?" their answer was "We are working on it." That response signaled right away that this was not a relationship built on a solid foundation. Although trust can sometimes be repaired if it is broken, it needs to be in place to begin with. All relationships require a foundation of trust, respect, and support. If any of these foundational elements are missing, consider working to establish them. Professional intervention can be extremely helpful. Counseling and therapy should not be seen as stigmas marking your relationships as broken; rather, they should be seen as a healthy approach to establishing a strong base.

Climb One Step at a Time

To prevent missteps, climb toward a higher perspective with consistent, steady, incremental steps. Don't risk a fall by trying to leap over rungs or perform fancy acrobatics to get attention. Healthy relationship habits rarely gain attention: drama and chaos are always more popular in the media. As a result, people tend to replicate toxic and unhealthy relationship patterns on the false premise that they are keeping things interesting. We jump from rung to rung haphazardly, thinking of our behavior as normal. Instead, it's better to follow incremental, disciplined relationship habits that help us gain elevation safely.

Lauren: Being an avid fitness enthusiast, I have tried almost every fitness trend. As a child, I dabbled in soccer, dance, gymnastics, swimming, golf, tennis, and karate. As I aged out of team sports, I tried spin classes, boxing gyms, and yoga. I was first introduced to CrossFit a few weeks after my son was born, at a time when I was exhausted, sleep-deprived, and craving the endorphins that come with vigorous exercise. Friends raved about the CrossFit culture and invited me to tag along for a WOD (a CrossFit acronym for "workout of the day").

Walking in, I noticed that the coach was close to my age and petite height, yet she had the strength of an ox. I watched as she stacked weights onto a bar and swept it from the ground up over her head in one graceful movement. At that point I did not feel strong enough to lift a fifteen-pound kettle bell, let alone raise my body weight over my head. She finished her set, walked over, introduced herself as Kim, and asked me if I wanted to try lifting some weights.

"Sure, but I must warn you, I probably need to start with just the bar." Kim helped me position my feet and hands and talked me through each movement. I practiced the lift with a piece of white PVC pipe, and then it was time to try it with the heavy metal bar. *I am about to make a fool of myself,* I thought.

"You are so ready!" Kim told me. "Just one last thing before you try it. I want you to picture yourself holding the bar over your head before you start the movement."

I closed my eyes and saw myself in a power pose of victory. If I could carry a toddler on one hip and an infant car seat on the other arm, I told myself, I could easily lift this bar. Kim counted down, "Three, two one — snatch!" With one swift movement, I lifted the bar from the ground to the sky. It felt amazing.

This launched me into a season as a CrossFit groupie. I joined the gym and carefully followed the coaches' instructions for making steady, gradual progress, ensuring I increased my challenges at a healthy and beneficial pace. Muscle growth occurs when the fibers sustain tiny injuries and then heal themselves. Incremental progress leads to healthy and sustained development, but overexertion or sudden tension can cause injuries. It's also important to prepare your body for the physical challenge with adequate nutrition, hydration, and sleep. And when you lift that bar, it requires complete focus. Consider the same discipline of small, incremental progress to gain perspective and strengthen relationships. Be honest, show up, turn off your phone, ask questions, be respectful, avoid putdowns, be helpful, and stay positive. Healthy discipline and routine practice strengthen your relational muscle fibers.

Keep Looking Up

Lauren: I am terrified of heights and would not find jumping out of a plane as exhilarating as my mom did. If you are anything like me, you can still experience the sensation that a little distance can bring without having to jump out of a plane. When flying, I prefer a window seat. As the plane lifts away from the tarmac and the wheels retract, I watch as the objects on the ground seem to shrink in size. Massive semi trucks begin to resemble the miniature trucks I collected as a kid. Acres of land start to look like a patchwork quilt. Interstate highways look like contour lines on a map. From thirty thousand feet up I can survey mountain ranges, ocean waters, and cotton-candy cloud formations. The beauty of our world captivates my soul. From this height, I realize that I am not alone: I am a part of something much bigger than myself or my circumstances. Whatever anxiety may be weighing me down loses its power as I view the big picture. Upward focus brings new perspective.

Looking up and outward reminds us of what is most important in life. If you are constantly looking down, staring at the messes your kids leave on the floor, try to look up and see them smile. If you find yourself obsessively comparing your social life to people's perfect lives on social media, look up from your screen and pursue real connection. If you habitually work late to crank out one more sale at the office, look up at the eyes of the people whose company you are missing. Although you cannot hop onto a plane every time you need this reminder, you can commit to always looking up.

When relationships feel heavy or the weight of stress has you running from people rather than toward them, grab your Extension Ladder to gain some distance from the ground-level drama. Remember to establish a secure foundation, climb one step at a time, and keep looking up. The view from a higher perspective helps us see that success in life is not measured by the quantity of money in our bank accounts, but rather by the quality of our relationships.

The Extended View

Joneen: I never used to believe people when they said, "Age is just a number" until I was approaching a milestone birthday. To celebrate, my husband staged a party emulating one of entertainment's very first reality TV shows, *This Is Your Life*. The show, which won two Emmy awards, aired on NBC radio from 1948 to 1952, and then on NBC television from 1952 to 1961. Originally hosted by its creator and producer, Ralph Edwards, the program surprised guests with a movie reel of highlights from their lives, projected in front of a studio audience. Colleagues, friends, and family of the guests appeared from behind a curtain.

My birthday surprise started with a delightful dinner date, and then my husband, Bruce, drove me to an undisclosed destination. I am always up for an adventure and joyfully went along for the ride. "We're here," Bruce said as we pulled into a parking lot. "Close your eyes and follow me." To ensure I did not peek, he gently tied a bandanna around my eyes. Holding my hand, he guided me indoors and up a short staircase. A bright light penetrated my blindfold, and I heard Bruce say, "Okay, Joneen. Open your eyes!" As I removed the bandanna, I saw that I was on a stage with hundreds of people sitting in the audience. Bruce took the microphone and played the role of the host. "Joneen Mackenzie, this is your life!"

Bruce gave a brief account of my childhood, my family tree, and a few of the milestones we had shared during our marriage. Then, one by one, people from all stages of my life came onstage: my mom and brothers, friends from college, Air Force roommates, and colleagues from every stage of my career. They shared treasured memories from the times we had together, and the audience erupted in laughter and tears.

How did I get so lucky? Mainly because my life was rich with relationships. Standing on the stage and looking back on my life's journey, I saw connection. This view from the top served as a reminder that nurturing the people in my life is my first and most important priority. Standing at the top of your Extension Ladder, what type of relationship legacy do you hope to see? If you have ever experienced the loss of a loved one, you understand the difficulty and sadness that ensues as a result. But loss also provides an exceptional opportunity for establishing higher perspective.

Lauren: Years ago we learned that my grandfather, Joneen's father-in-law, had suffered a stroke. His doctors informed us that our hospital visit would likely be our last chance to see him and encouraged us to say our goodbyes. We were grateful for the chance to visit him, yet filled with grief.

The stroke had robbed Grandpa of his short-term memory, but, thankfully, he maintained his long-term recollections. I wanted to capture every last bit of his wisdom. I will always remember a conversation we shared in the hospital courtyard. "Grandpa," I asked, "from your perspective, what made your life such a great success?" He sat quietly for a few moments, pondering his answer. I waited patiently, noticing how the sunlight framed his face.

"Success is about hard work," he responded. "Ambition is important too. If you work hard and have ambition, you will achieve great things." As his eyes met mine, I saw great pride in his countenance and felt the passion behind his answer. He had been a talented and successful architect. Grandpa was leaving us a legacy built on discipline, work ethic, and ambition.

"I love that, Grandpa," I replied. "I see all of those amazing character qualities in you. Would it be okay if I added one more observation?" He looked at me and nodded. "There is something I have noticed about your time in this hospital. Every day, your room is filled with visitors and people who love you. You are so loved, Grandpa. To me, this is the most critical indicator of your life's success."

We sat in that moment with no further agenda, nowhere to be, and no pressing tasks to attend to. We were together, and that was all that mattered. This conversation left an imprint on my heart. When my last days are approaching, who will stop by the hospital desk for a visitor's badge? Will I have a track record of loving people well or causing hurt and pain? Will any of the visitors' faces hide resentment or regrets? These are heavy questions, but questions we must ask. They help us focus on what is important and remind us to climb toward successful connections. When we place too much emphasis on the here and now, we can forget to consider the then and there.

Stepping up on our Extension Ladder reminds us to consider the implications of present actions and decisions that can help or hurt us in the long run.

TAKEAWAY TOOL SUMMARY

Sometimes stress and hardship feel impossible to manage. To cope, we tend to seek refuge in isolation and avoid the work required to maintain relationships. Withdrawing, however, is not the answer. Our burdens get even heavier when we try to carry them alone. Instead of distancing from others, seek to gain perspective on ground-level circumstances by ascending higher and expanding your view. Make sure your Extension Ladder is set on a firm foundation, climb one step at a time, and keep looking up. Sometimes focusing on the long term can bring clarity: consider the legacy you will leave. Life success is not measured by our accomplishments but rather by the quality of our relationships.

CONCLUSION

Relationship Essentials
Toolkit Checklist

Reading *Relationship Essentials* has equipped you with practical tools to stock in your toolbox for building meaningful connections. Each one can aid you in constructing, maintaining, or repairing relationships with the people in your life. With the right tools, any task feels easier. Use your toolbox to build something beautiful!

❏ **Power Drill:** Enable powerful and complete connection by breaking communication down into three specific components: *content, context,* and *connection.* All three must work together like three interdependent components of a power drill.

❏ **Flashlight:** Shine a spotlight on others and learn to take a genuine interest in them.

❏ **Tape Measure:** Learn to measure and mark your personal boundaries.

❏ **Adjustable Wrench:** Establish the nuts and bolts of your expectations, and widen or narrow your grip when identifying the disappointment of an expectation gap.

❏ **Safety Glasses:** Protect your relationships by learning to reframe conflict and see it through a positive lens.

❏ **Hammer:** Aim to do things purposefully, with discipline and a plan. Intentionality will help you achieve meaningful connection and avoid leaving relational success to chance.

❏ **Spirit Level:** Learn to find balance among differences, and value respect over being right.

❏ **Scissors:** Cut it out with the excuses and own your mistakes!

❏ **Battery:** Charge your relationships with gratitude, which enhances both energy and positivity in relationships.

❏ **Extension Ladder:** Distance yourself from everyday stress to gain a higher perspective and keep relationship success in sight.

NOTES

Chapter 1: The Three *C*'s of Communication

p. 3   *"The cerebral cortex"*: "What Is the Memory Capacity of a Human Brain?," CNS West, Clinical Neurology Specialists, March 13, 2020, https://www.cnsnevada.com/what-is-the-memory-capacity-of-a-human-brain/.

p. 5   *the surprising ways people ask dates to a high school prom*: "What Does 'Promposal' Mean?," Merriam-Webster, n.d., https://www.merriam-webster.com/words-at-play/what-does-promposal-mean.

p. 5   *according to a survey of 1,155 teens*: Alisson Clark, "Asking Out a Prom Date Via Text? 40 Percent of Teens Say Yes," *Wired*, June 3, 2017, https://www.wired.com/2011/04/asking-out-a-prom-date-via-text-40-percent-of-teens-say-yes/.

p. 6   *the mere presence of mobile phones during interactions*: Andrew K. Przybylski and Netta Weinstein, "Can You Connect with Me Now? How the Presence of Mobile Communication Technology Influences Face-to-Face Conversation Quality," *Journal of Social and Personal Relationships*, July 19, 2012, https://journals.sagepub.com/doi/full/10.1177/0265407512453827.

p. 6   *"a face-to-face interaction is 34 times more successful"*: Vanessa K. Bohns, "A Face-to-Face Request Is 34 Times More Successful Than an Email," *Harvard Business Review*, January 26, 2018, https://hbr.org/2017/04/a-face-to-face-request-is-34-times-more-successful-than-an-email.

p. 12   *"a key ingredient of successful relationships"*: Quoted in "The Psychology of Emotional and Cognitive Empathy," Lesley University, n.d., https://lesley.edu/article/the-psychology-of-emotional-and-cognitive-empathy.

p. 12   *the Speaker Listener Technique*: Howard J. Markman, Scott M. Stanley, and Susan L. Blumberg, *Fighting for Your Marriage* (San Francisco:

Jossey-Bass, 2010). To view a video about this technique, search for "The Speaker Listener Technique" on YouTube.

Chapter 2: Getting to Know All about You

p. 19   *"The pure effort of that, the 'getting to know you' quality"*: Jeff Lunden, "Getting to Know the Real Story Was Key to Broadway's 'King and I' Revival," NPR, May 2, 2015, https://www.npr.org/2015/05/02/403047081/getting -to-know-the-real-story-was-key-to-broadway-s-king-and-i-revival.

p. 21   *"Research has found people who are inquisitive"*: Stephanie Vozza, "How the Most Successful People Ask Questions," *Fast Company*, February 5, 2016, https://www.fastcompany.com/3056318/how-the-most-successful -people-ask-questions.

p. 25   *"people do feel more socially connected"*: Jenny Anderson, "Do Lots of Chats with Strangers or a Few Deep Conversations with Friends Make You Happier?," Quartz, September 30, 2019, https://qz.com/1715913 /does-small-talk-or-deep-conversations-make-us-happier/.

p. 26   *"relating to or involving the imagination"*: Lexico.com, s.v. "creative," n.d., https://www.lexico.com/en/definition/creative.

p. 27   *"deciding that something or someone"*: *Cambridge English Dictionary*, s.v. "dismissing," n.d., https://dictionary.cambridge.org/us/dictionary /english/dismissing.

p. 28   *"When we are not engaged in thinking about some definite problem"*: Dale Carnegie, *How to Win Friends and Influence People* (New York: Simon and Schuster, 2011), chapter 2.

p. 30   *"Putting others first is a form of enlightened self-concern"*: Michael McGee, "Put Others First," Dr. Michael McGee, n.d., https://drmichael mcgee.com/put-others-first/.

Chapter 3: Enough Is Enough

p. 35   *an educational researcher set out to evaluate the behavior*: See Will Krieger, "Lessons from the Playground," Repass, April 28, 2016, http:// repassinc.com/2016/04/4125/.

Chapter 4: Tell Me What You Want

p. 50   *"If you want to make a difference in the world"*: Daniela Pierre-Bravo, "Why Making Your Bed Can Change Your Life," NBCNews.com, May 30, 2018, https://www.nbcnews.com/know-your-value/feature/why -making-your-bed-can-change-your-life-ncna829446.

Chapter 5: Giving It a Fighting Chance

p. 62 *"In Mandarin, the following words are used"*: Bao Yingshan, "The Research of Interpersonal Conflict and Solution Strategies," *Psychology* 7, no. 14 (April 2016), https://www.scirp.org/journal/paperinformation.aspx?paperid=65687.

p. 64 *"a close, familiar, and usually affectionate"*: Dictionary.com, s.v., "intimacy," n.d., https://www.dictionary.com/browse/intimacy.

p. 67 *"During a fight-flight-freeze response"*: Kirsten Nunez, "Fight, Flight, Freeze: What This Response Means," Healthline, February 21, 2020, https://www.healthline.com/health/mental-health/fight-flight-freeze.

p. 72 *"Not only do negative events and experiences imprint more quickly"*: Margaret Jaworski, "The Negativity Bias: Why the Bad Stuff Sticks and How to Overcome It," Psycom.net, February 19, 2020, https://www.psycom.net/negativity-bias.

Chapter 6: Nailed It!

p. 75 *"our [human] need to connect"*: Quoted in Gareth Cook, "Why We Are Wired to Connect," *Scientific American*, October 22, 2013, https://www.scientificamerican.com/article/why-we-are-wired-to-connect/.

p. 82 *the average adult makes about thirty-five thousand remotely conscious decisions*: Frank Graff, "How Many Daily Decisions Do We Make?" UNC TV Science blog, February 2018, http://science.unctv.org/content/reportersblog/choices.

p. 84 *These include executive function*: "Know Your Brain: Prefrontal Cortex," Neuroscientifically Challenged, January 4, 2021, https://www.neuroscientificallychallenged.com/blog/2014/5/16/know-your-brain-prefrontal-cortex.

Chapter 7: Finding Equilibrium

p. 91 *rapid ascent from a dive is dangerous*: "Pressure Injuries from Scuba Diving," Michigan Medicine, n.d., https://www.uofmhealth.org/health-library/abo0894.

p. 92 *the work of John Trent and Gary Smalley*: "Gary Smalley and Dr. John Trent's Personality Inventory," n.d., http://www.nacada.ksu.edu/Portals/0/CandIGDivision/documents/2014AC%20-%20Smalley%20Personality%20Inventory.pdf.

p. 96 *River otters have been observed to build slides*: "16 Playful Facts about Otters," Mental Floss, June 26, 2018, https://www.mentalfloss.com/article/548648/facts-about-otters.

p. 96   *Sea otters love to stay close together*: "Otters," Animals, National Geographic, February 21, 2019, https://www.nationalgeographic.com/animals/mammals/facts/otters-1.

p. 99   *"Beaver dams do not just create a place for beavers to live"*: "Build a Beaver Dam," National Park Service, U.S. Department of the Interior, n.d., https://www.nps.gov/articles/buildabeaverdam.htm.

Chapter 9: Gratitude's Superpower

p. 121   *Sometimes a sense of entitlement can emerge*: F. Diane Barth, "What Makes Some People Feel Entitled to Special Treatment?" *Psychology Today*, October 19, 2013, https://www.psychologytoday.com/us/blog/the-couch/201310/what-makes-some-people-feel-entitled-special-treatment.

p. 122   *all the trees in a forest are interconnected*: Brigit Katz, "Pando, One of the World's Largest Organisms, Is Dying," Smithsonian Institution, October 18, 2018, https://www.smithsonianmag.com/smart-news/pano-one-worlds-largest-organisms-dying-180970579/.

p. 128   *"As [Eagles quarterback Nick] Foles stood for his interview"*: Justin Bariso, "Super Bowl MVP Nick Foles's Post-game Interview Is a Powerful Lesson in Leadership," Inc., February 5, 2018, https://www.inc.com/justin-bariso/super-bowl-mvp-nick-foles-post-game-interview-powerful-lesson-leadership.html.

p. 128   *"Social scientists have been studying gratitude"*: Robert H. Frank, "Why Luck Matters — Much More Than You Think," *The Atlantic*, October 24, 2016, https://www.theatlantic.com/magazine/archive/2016/05/why-luck-matters-more-than-you-might-think/476394/.

Chapter 10: The View from the Top

p. 134   *"More than a quarter of people in a recent survey felt alienated"*: Kira M. Newman, "Could Stress Be Causing Your Relationship Problems?" Greater Good Magazine, n.d., https://greatergood.berkeley.edu/article/item/could_stress_be_causing_your_relationship_problems.

p. 134   *"the muscles that control the shape of the lens"*: Danielle Haak, "Accommodation Reflex of the Eye: Definition and Purpose," Study.com, February 4, 2021, https://study.com/academy/lesson/accommodation-reflex-of-the-eye-definition-purpose.html.

p. 139   *The show, which won two Emmy awards*: "This Is Your Life," Wikipedia, n.d., http://en.wikipedia.org/wiki/This_Is_Your_Life.

ABOUT THE AUTHORS

Lauren Reitsema is vice president of strategy and communications at The Center for Relationship Education. Her interest in relationship skills began when her parents divorced after almost twenty years of marriage. Seeking to acquire skills to prepare for and safeguard her own future legacy, she earned her bachelor's degree in communications and graduated as the Guild Scholar of the College of Communications at Texas Christian University. Lauren is also the author of *In Their Shoes*, a book dedicated to helping parents and stepparents understand the impact that divorce has on children. Additionally, she is coauthor of the REAL Essentials curriculum, CRE's relationship education skills program. Her professional speaking career has spanned more than fifteen years, teaching young people, adults, and corporate teams purposeful and practical relationship skills. She and her husband love adventuring with their three children. Native to Colorado, they are avid skiers, outdoor enthusiasts, and Broncos fans.

Joneen Mackenzie is the president and founder of The Center for Relationship Education, which has pioneered training resources in the field of relationship education for more than twenty-five years. She developed the foundational framework of the nationally acclaimed REAL Essentials curriculum and has certified thousands of educators to empower participants to build and maintain healthy relationships. A graduate of the University of Texas, Joneen is a registered nurse and a former first lieutenant in the US Air Force Nurse Corps. Her credentials in public health make her a valued member of national boards, including the National Association of Relationship and Marriage Education (NARME), and a contributor to public policy regarding relational health. She is also a member of the Human Flourishing Program's Community of Practice at Harvard University. Joneen is the mother of four grown children and has a special knack for initiating belly laughs in her grandchildren. She loves traveling with her husband and experiencing new cultures and traditions around the world. She lives in Colorado.

THE CENTER FOR RELATIONSHIP EDUCATION AND REAL ESSENTIALS CERTIFICATION

Bring relationship skills to your community.

Become a REAL Essentials Certified Educator

REAL Essentials is the premier program for educators and training professionals who seek effective, scalable solutions for relationship education and interpersonal skills training.

For Schools and Parents

REAL Essentials Foundations

Customized curricula designed to reach elementary, middle school, and high school students as well as adults in college or postgraduate studies. Curriculum is also available for providing relationship skills to single-parent and co-parenting families.

For Emergency Responder and Military Agencies

REAL Essentials Respond

Specialized training tailored to the specific relational needs of emergency responder and military personnel.

For Individuals, Corporate Teams, and Couples

REAL Essentials Connect

Training designed to equip community and corporate educators with resources for enhancing relationship skills in the community, the workplace, and the family.

The Center for Relationship Education (CRE) is committed to bringing foundational relationship skills to people of all ages and walks of life to create understanding and effective communication in workplaces, schools, and homes across the globe.

About The Center for Relationship Education

The Center for Relationship Education shines a spotlight on the role that successful relationships play in leading happy, healthy lives. CRE combines evidence-based, proven curricula with facilitator training and certification to bring relationship skills to more audiences to ultimately strengthen schools, workplaces, and communities. CRE is committed to expanding relationship education by fulfilling social initiatives that enhance communication and understanding in key populations. Above all, the organization makes it simple and fun for anyone to learn more about themselves and how to enhance their relationships.

For more information, visit www.myrelationshipcenter.org.